MATH

Kindergarten

Credits
Author: Caroline Oliver Carpenter
Copy Editors: Elise Craver, Christine Schwab

Visit *carsondellosa.com* for correlations to Common Core, state, national, and Canadian provincial standards.

Carson-Dellosa Publishing, LLC
PO Box 35665
Greensboro, NC 27425 USA
carsondellosa.com

978-1-4838-2794-0
01-053167784

Table of Contents

Introduction

The Weekly Practice series provides 40 weeks of essential daily practice in either math or language arts. It is the perfect supplement to any classroom curriculum and provides standards-based activities for every day of the week but Friday.

The activities are intended as homework assignments for Monday through Thursday and cover a wide spectrum of standards-based skills. The skills are presented at random to provide comprehensive learning but are repeated systematically throughout the book. The intention is to offer regular, focused practice to ensure mastery and retention.

Each 192-page book provides 40 weeks of reproducible pages, a standards alignment matrix, flash cards, and an answer key. The reproducible pages are perfect for homework but also work well for morning work, early finishers, and warm-up activities.

About This Book

Each page contains a variety of short, fun exercises that build in difficulty across the span of the book. The activities are divided into two sections:

- The Daily Extension Activities at the front of the book are intended to engage both student and family. These off-the-page activities are simple and fun so that students will look forward to this practice time at home. The activities span one week at a time. The instructions are clear and simple so that students can follow them with or without assistance in their homes. None need be returned to school.

- The daily practice section involves more comprehensive learning. Because of the simplicity of directions and straightforward tasks, students will be able to complete most tasks independently in a short period of time. There are four pages of activities per week, allowing for testing or a student break on Friday if desired. These pages are intended to be brought back to school.

Pages can be offered in any order, making it possible to reinforce specific skills when needed. However, skills are repeated regularly throughout the book to ensure retention over time, making a strong case for using pages sequentially.

An answer key is included for the daily practice section. You can check answers as a group for a quick follow-up lesson or monitor students' progress individually. Follow the basic page layout provided at the beginning of the answer key to match answers to page placement. Also included in the book is a set of flash cards. Reproduce them to give to students for at-home practice, or place them in classroom centers.

Common Core State Standards Alignment Matrix

Standard	W1	W2	W3	W4	W5	W6	W7	W8	W9	W10	W11	W12	W13	W14	W15	W16	W17	W18	W19	W20
K.CC.A.1	•	•	•	•	•	•	•	•	•	•	•	•	•	•	•	•	•	•	•	•
K.CC.A.2	•	•	•	•	•	•				•	•	•	•							
K.CC.A.3	•	•	•	•	•	•	•	•		•	•	•				•			•	•
K.CC.B.4	•	•	•	•	•	•	•	•	•	•	•	•	•		•	•	•	•	•	•
K.CC.B.5	•	•	•	•	•	•	•	•	•	•	•	•			•	•	•	•	•	•
K.CC.C.6										•	•	•	•	•	•	•	•			
K.CC.C.7												•	•	•	•			•		
K.OA.A.1															•	•	•	•	•	
K.OA.A.2															•	•			•	
K.OA.A.3									•											
K.OA.A.4																				•
K.OA.A.5																				•
K.NBT.A.1											•			•			•			•
K.MD.A.1	•		•	•	•	•	•	•	•	•	•	•	•			•	•	•	•	•
K.MD.A.2	•	•	•	•	•	•	•	•	•	•	•	•	•	•		•	•	•	•	•
K.MD.B.3		•			•	•		•	•			•	•		•		•	•	•	•
K.G.A.1	•	•	•	•	•	•	•	•	•	•							•	•	•	
K.G.A.2	•			•	•	•	•	•	•	•			•		•	•		•		•
K.G.A.3	•					•	•	•	•										•	
K.G.B.4						•				•	•	•	•	•	•		•	•	•	•
K.G.B.5		•															•			
K.G.B.6										•				•						

W = Week

Common Core State Standards Alignment Matrix

Standard	W21	W22	W23	W24	W25	W26	W27	W28	W29	W30	W31	W32	W33	W34	W35	W36	W37	W38	W39	W40
K.CC.A.1	●	●	●	●	●	●	●	●	●	●	●	●	●	●	●	●	●	●	●	●
K.CC.A.2	●	●			●	●	●	●						●						
K.CC.A.3	●	●	●	●	●	●	●	●			●									
K.CC.B.4	●	●		●			●	●	●	●	●					●				
K.CC.B.5	●	●	●		●		●			●	●	●	●							
K.CC.C.6	●	●	●	●		●	●	●												
K.CC.C.7	●	●	●	●			●	●												
K.OA.A.1	●		●	●	●	●	●	●	●	●	●	●	●	●	●	●	●		●	●
K.OA.A.2	●		●	●	●	●	●	●	●	●	●	●	●	●	●		●	●	●	
K.OA.A.3	●		●	●	●			●	●	●	●	●	●	●	●	●	●			
K.OA.A.4	●		●	●		●	●	●	●	●	●	●	●	●	●	●	●	●	●	●
K.OA.A.5								●	●	●	●	●	●	●	●	●	●	●	●	●
K.NBT.A.1		●	●	●	●	●				●		●	●		●	●	●	●	●	●
K.MD.A.1	●					●		●	●	●	●	●	●		●		●			
K.MD.A.2	●					●				●		●								
K.MD.B.3					●	●														
K.G.A.1	●																			
K.G.A.2		●																●		●
K.G.A.3	●													●				●		
K.G.B.4		●	●	●	●	●	●	●		●		●		●		●	●	●		●
K.G.B.5	●	●	●	●	●	●		●		●		●						●		
K.G.B.6			●	●	●	●	●		●			●		●		●				●

W = Week

School to Home Communication

The research is clear that family involvement is strongly linked to student success. Support for student learning at home improves student achievement in school. Educators should not underestimate the significance of this connection.

The activities in this book create an opportunity to create or improve this school-to-home link. The activities span a week at a time and can be sent home as a week-long homework packet each Monday. Simply clip together the strip of fun activities from the front of the book with the pages for Days 1 to 4 for the correct week.

Most of the activities can be completed independently, but many encourage feedback or interaction with a family member. The activities are simple and fun, aiming to create a brief pocket of learning that is enjoyable to all.

In order to make the school-to-home program work for students and their families, we encourage you to reach out to them with an introductory letter. Explain the program and its intent and ask them to partner with you in their children's educational process. Describe the role you expect them to play. Encourage them to offer suggestions or feedback along the way.

A sample letter is included below. Use it as is or create your own letter to introduce this project and elicit their collaboration.

Dear Families,

I anticipate a productive and exciting year of learning and look forward to working with you and your child. We have a lot of work to do! I hope we—teacher, student, and family—can work together as a team to achieve the goal of academic progress we all hope for this year.

I will send home a packet of homework each week on _____. There will be two items to complete each day: a single task on a strip plus a full page of focused practice. Each page or strip is labeled Day 1 (for Monday), Day 2, Day 3, or Day 4. There is no homework on Friday.

Please make sure that your student brings back the completed work _____. It is important that these are brought in on time as we may work on some of the lessons as a class.

If you have any questions about this program or would like to talk to me about it, please feel free to call or email me. Thank you for joining me in making this the best year ever for your student!

Sincerely,

_____
Name

_____
Phone

_____
Email

	Day 1	Day 2	Day 3	Day 4
Week 1	How many letters are in your first name? Practice writing that number.	Find three circles in your home. Draw one of them.	Fill two cups with water. Lift up each cup. Tell which one is heavier. Repeat the activity using different cups.	Use small objects such as coins to build sets. Build a set to represent each number from one to five.

	Day 1	Day 2	Day 3	Day 4
Week 2	How many letters are in your last name? Practice writing that number.	Have an adult place flour in the bottom of a baking pan Practice tracing a circle, rectangle, square, and triangle with your finger in the flour.	Cut a piece of string to a certain length. Use it to compare things around your home. What is longer? Shorter? The same length?	Cut out the numbers 0 to 5 from a magazine or newspaper. Glue them to a sheet of paper in the correct order.

	Day 1	Day 2	Day 3	Day 4
Week 3	Choose five of your toys. Arrange them in a single line. Point to each toy as you count it aloud.	Practice writing the numbers 0 to 5. Ask someone to write each number on an index card. Then, trace the numbers with different colors of markers.	On a sheet of paper, write the number 5. Underneath it, draw a set of five objects and write the number word five.	Use sidewalk chalk to draw a large square. Walk around the square. Count the sides.

	Day 1	Day 2	Day 3	Day 4
Week 4	Practice writing the numbers 5 to 10. Ask someone to write each number on an index card. Then, trace the numbers with different colors of markers.	Roll a die. Count the dots on top. Write the number. Continue rolling and writing until you have written all of the numbers from 1 to 6.	Have an adult write the numbers 1 to 5 on sheets of paper. Use play dough to form each number. Use the written numbers as guides to form each number with play dough.	Have an adult draw a large triangle on a sheet of paper. Trace the triangle. Count the sides. Write the number of sides inside the triangle.

	Day 1	Day 2	Day 3	Day 4
Week 5	Have an adult write the numbers *5* to *10* on sheets of paper. Use play dough to form each number. Use the written numbers as guides to form each number with play dough.	Choose a pair of stuffed animals. Tell which animal is taller and which one is shorter.	Put a small handful of cereal on the table. Count the pieces of cereal and write the number. Repeat with another handful of cereal. Which handful of cereal was larger?	Choose a small toy. Have an adult call out directions telling you where to put the toy. For example: *Put the toy under the chair.* Or, *put the toy next to the book.*

	Day 1	Day 2	Day 3	Day 4
Week 6	Draw 10 balloons. Label the balloons with the numbers *1* to *10*.	Have an adult cut out four different shapes from paper. Talk about what makes the shapes similar and different.	Cut off two sections of the end of an egg carton. Use fish crackers or marbles to show different numbers from 1 to 10 in your "ten frame."	Count to 10 while doing jumping jacks.

	Day 1	Day 2	Day 3	Day 4
Week 7	Find a ball and a coin. Tell which one is flat and which one is 3-D. Tell how they are alike and different.	How old are you? Write that number five times.	Have an adult draw a ten frame for you. Draw dots to show 10. Write the number *10* below the ten frame.	Collect a pile of paper clips. Collect a pile of coins. Tell which pile has more.

	Day 1	Day 2	Day 3	Day 4
Week 8	Count the number of chairs in your home. Rainbow write that number.	Hold out your arms and hold a bag of apples in each hand. Do the bags feel the same? Does one have more apples than the other? What can you do to make each bag feel the same?	Count items in your kitchen such as spoons, spatulas, and sponges. Which group has the most? Which group has the least?	Draw a rectangle. Count the sides. Circle the corners. Write the number of sides and corners below the rectangle.

	Day 1	Day 2	Day 3	Day 4
Week 9	Have an adult write the numbers *1* to *10* on index cards. Collect small items from around your home to build sets to represent each number.	Fold a piece of paper in half. On the left side, draw 2-D shapes. On the right, glue matching pictures of 3-D objects found in a magazine or newspaper.	Take off a shoe. Walk around your home and find things that are shorter than your shoe. Make a list.	Put 10 pieces of cereal on the table. Hide some of the cereal under a bowl. Tell the number you can see and the number that is hiding.

	Day 1	Day 2	Day 3	Day 4
Week 10	Count the number of people in your home. Use your finger to write that number in the air.	Go on a shapes scavenger hunt. Try to find at least three triangles, circles, and rectangles in your home.	Set the table. Count each object placed on the table.	Use popcorn to build sets of 5, 10, 15, and 20.

	Day 1	Day 2	Day 3	Day 4
Week 11	Ask a family member to count to 30 with you. Take turns saying each number.	Draw a picture of a boat using only rectangles and triangles.	Have an adult write the numbers *1* to *20* on small pieces of paper. Glue them in order on a large piece of paper.	Roll two dice from a board game. Count the dots. Write the number. Continue rolling and writing until you have written all of the numbers from *2* to *12*.

	Day 1	Day 2	Day 3	Day 4
Week 12	Count the number of animals in your home. How many are real? How many are toys? Do you have more real animals or toy animals?	Count the number of fruit snacks in a bag. Sort them by color. How many are in each group? Which group has the most?	Draw a large rectangle. Glue yarn onto the page to outline the rectangle. When the glue is dry, trace the shape with your finger. Tell how many sides and corners it has.	Look in your closet. Do you have more clothes or more shoes?

	Day 1	Day 2	Day 3	Day 4
Week 13	Count out three dried beans. Count out five dried beans. Which group has more? Have an adult make two more groups for you to count and compare.	Count from one to 10 while hopping on one foot. Switch feet and continue hopping and counting to 20.	Fill two resealable bags with two different snack items such as crackers or fruit. Compare the weight of each bag. Which bag is the heaviest? Which bag is the lightest?	Use toothpicks or pretzel sticks to make shapes. Make sure the sides touch end to end to make closed figures.

	Day 1	Day 2	Day 3	Day 4
Week 14	Drop five counters on a container lid. Record how many landed on the lid and how many landed off of it. Practice adding pairs of numbers that make five.	Use spoons to measure different objects in your home. Be sure to lay the spoons end to end when measuring. Record the measurements.	Use the number cards from a deck of cards. Shuffle the cards. Draw two cards. Compare the numbers. Is one larger? Are they equal?	Count the number of doors in your home. Write the number. Count the number of windows in your home. Write the number. Do you have more windows or doors?

	Day 1	Day 2	Day 3	Day 4
Week 15	Search your home for 3-D shapes. Try to find a cylinder, sphere, cone, and cube. Draw one of them.	Write the numbers *1* to *10* on a sheet of paper, placing two numbers on each line. Circle the greater number on each line. What did you notice?	Make a list of people you know. Count the number of girls on the list. Count the number of boys. Does the list have more boys or girls?	Collect 10 toys and arrange them in a line. Have an adult call out directions such as… *Point to the first toy* or *point the toy between the car and the bear.*

	Day 1	Day 2	Day 3	Day 4
Week 16	Help an adult put away dishes. Discuss how they are grouped in the drawers and on the shelves.	When taking a bath, fill three cups with water. Which one is the heaviest? Which one is the lightest? Place them in order from heaviest to lightest.	Sort your shoes. Count how many are in each group.	Collect 10 packages of food from the cupboard. Sort them by shape. Count the number of packages in each group.

	Day 1	Day 2	Day 3	Day 4
Week 17	Draw a picture of a chair in your home. Write words below the picture to describe the chair. Is it big or small? Soft or hard? What color is it?	Sort a handful of coins. Tell how you sorted them. Count the number of coins in each group. Tell one thing that the coins all have in common.	Choose four toys. Arrange the toys from tallest to shortest.	Have an adult write the numbers from 1 to 20, in any order, in a single column. Write the number that is one more beside each number.

	Day 1	Day 2	Day 3	Day 4
Week 18	Ask a family member to count to 60 with you. Take turns saying each number.	Roll two dice. Write a number sentence that matches the dots on the dice. Count the dots to solve the problem.	Have an adult write the numbers 1 to 10 pieces of masking tape and then place them on a rug. Jump from one number to the next in the correct order.	Cut out two lily pads from paper or felt. Use counters or green marbles for frogs. Practice putting frogs on the lily pads. Tell which lily pad has more and which has less.

	Day 1	Day 2	Day 3	Day 4
Week 19	Write your name. Write the name of a family member. Count the letters in each name and write the numbers. Whose name has more letters?	Find different measuring tools in your kitchen such as measuring cups, measuring spoons, a scale, etc. Talk with an adult about what types of things are measured with each one.	Have an adult fill a resealable plastic bag halfway with glue or paint. Seal it, removing the air. Tape the bag to a window or glass door. Use your finger to "draw" different shapes on the bag.	Sort the socks in your sock drawer. Tell how you sorted them. Do you have more of one kind of sock than another?

	Day 1	Day 2	Day 3	Day 4
Week 20	Find 10 small toys in your room. Sort them. Count them. Discuss how many are in each group. How are the toys you grouped together the same?	Find five books. Line them up in order from shortest to tallest.	Roll a die. Write the number. How many more to make 10? Write the number. Continue rolling and writing until you have six pairs of numbers that make 10.	Use pieces of cereal to form different shapes. Tell how many sides and corners each shape has.

	Day 1	Day 2	Day 3	Day 4
Week 21	Ask a family member to count by 2s to 20 with you. Take turns saying each number.	Draw a picture of your school using only circles, squares, rectangles, and triangles.	Write your phone number five times.	Stand at one end of the room. Count your steps aloud as you walk across the room. How many steps did you take? Jump and count back to the other side. How many jumps did it take?

	Day 1	Day 2	Day 3	Day 4
Week 22	Count the number of doorknobs in your home. What number is one more? What number is one less?	Measure your favorite book using paper clips. Be sure to lay the paper clips end to end.	Put 10 apple fish crackers on a plate. Push some to one side and some to the other. Tell what you need to do to make both sides equal.	Put two handfuls of uncooked pasta noodles on the table. Arrange each pile into a line. Which line is longer? Count the number of noodles in each line.

	Day 1	Day 2	Day 3	Day 4
Week 23	Hunt for shapes in a book. Look for circles, triangles, and squares.	Ask an adult to draw a large triangle and a large square. Cut them out and combine them to make another shape.	Ask a family member to count by 10s to 100 with you. Take turns saying each number.	Trace both hands on 10 sheet of paper. On one sheet, color one finger blue. Color the remaining fingers red. Repeat with all of the number pairs that make 10 (2 and 8, 3 and 7, etc.).

	Day 1	Day 2	Day 3	Day 4
Week 24	Build a house using toothpicks and miniature marshmallows. Tell about the shapes you made.	Choose a number from one to 10. Use two different colors of interlocking plastic blocks to build the number. How many ways can you show the number?	Draw a train using only rectangles, squares, and circles.	Use spaghetti noodles as tens rods and macaroni noodles as ones blocks. Ask an adult to write the numbers 11 to 20 on index cards. Use the noodles to show how many tens and ones in each number.

	Day 1	Day 2	Day 3	Day 4
Week 25	Draw 3 triangles. Tell how they are the same and how they are different.	Draw a circle, rectangle, square, and triangle. Find examples of related 3-D shapes in your home for each one (sphere, cube, cone, and rectangular prism).	Write the numbers 11 to 20 on index cards. Link paper clips to represent each number. Clip each string of paper clips to the correct index card.	Ask a family member to count by 5s to 100 with you. Take turns saying each number.
Week 26	Use play dough and toothpicks or straws to create a cube. Count the number of faces, edges, and corners.	Make a list of things you can eat that are shaped like a cylinder.	Roll a die. Count how many. Draw a shape with that many sides. Continue rolling and drawing until you have drawn six different shapes.	Ask an adult to cut out several small shapes. Glue them to a paper plate to create a shape pizza. Count the number of each "topping" on your pizza.
Week 27	Have an adult use coins or counters to cover five numbers on a calendar. Study the calendar and tell what numbers are covered.	Put three toys on the floor. Then, add four more. How many toys are on the floor now? Repeat the activity with different amounts of toys.	Make a list of all of the spheres you can find in your home.	Count the number of forks in your kitchen. Count the number of spoons in your kitchen. How many forks and spoons do you have altogether?
Week 28	Have an adult use sidewalk chalk to draw a number line labeled from 0 to 10. Stand on a number. Have an adult call out directions such as *two more* or *three less*. Hop to the correct number.	Look for a sporting event in the news. Ask an adult to write the scores. Tell how many tens and ones are in each number.	Use a shoe box to make a mailbox. Have an adult cut a slot in the top. Use playing cards as "envelopes." Count the number of envelopes as you place them in the slot.	Place five crackers on a plate. Take some away. How many crackers are left? Repeat the activity, taking away different amounts of crackers each time.

	Day 1	Day 2	Day 3	Day 4
Week 29	Play a number riddle game on the way to school. Spy something and have an adult guess how many of there are the item.	Cut out 10 shapes from a newpaper or magazine. Sort them into two groups: flat shapes and 3-D shapes.	Have an adult tie yarn together to make two circles. Pour a small scoop of cereal onto the table. Use the yarn to circle groups of 10. Starting with the tens, count the pieces of cereal.	Count the number of people who live in your home. How many legs do they have altogether?
Week 30	Pick a number from 1 to 10. Look through a magazine or catalog. Find and cut out pictures that show the number. Make a collage of the pictures you find.	Write the numbers from *1* to *5* on the sections of a beach ball. Toss the ball with a family member. When you catch it, tell the sum of the numbers your thumbs are touching.	Clap your hands as you skip count by 10s to 100.	Use crayons to measure three obejcts in your home. Draw a picture of the objects in order from shortest to longest.
Week 31	Count out ten crackers. Give some to a family member. How many crackers do you have left?	Write the number *10* on a paper plate and place it on the table. Put two paper plates below it. Put some pasta noodles on the first plate. Put enough pasta noodles on the second plate to make a total of 10.	Draw a circle on a sheet of paper. Drop five dried beans onto the circle. Count how many beans landed outside of the circle. Write a number sentence to describe the numbers. For example, *5 – 3 = 2.*	Use play dough to form 3-D shapes. Make a sphere, cone, and cube.
Week 32	Think of an addition number sentence. Draw a picture to match. For example, *5 frogs were sitting on a log. 3 more frogs came along. This picture matches 5 + 3 = 8.*	Start with a pile of crackers. Take 10. Label a die with *+1, +2, +3, –1, –2,* and *–3* on the sides. Roll the die. Add or take that many crackers. After five rolls, how many crackers do you have left?	Have an adult write the numbers and sets to match each number for *1* to *10* on self-stick notes. Have her stick the notes around your home. See how fast you can find all of the matches.	With help from an adult, sort items from your recycling bin by shape. What shapes did you find?

14

	Day 1	Day 2	Day 3	Day 4
Week 33	Choose two number cards from a deck of playing cards. Write an addition number sentence and find the sum. Count the objects on the cards to check your work.	Use your toys to act out number stories. For example, *I have 5 cars. 3 of them drove away. I have 2 cars left.*	Stomp your feet as you skip count by 5s to 100.	Make a list of three objects in your home that are shorter than you and three objects that are taller than you.
Week 34	Draw a picture of your room. Tell about the objects in your room using shapes. For example, *My bed is a rectangle.*	Make a ten frame by taping 10 plastic cups together. Put a small toy in each cup. Take one away. Count how many are left. Continue removing toys and counting until there are none left.	Fill three measuring cups with uncooked rice. Lift each one. Which is the lightest? Which is the heaviest? Arrange the cups in order from lightest to heaviest.	Use three bracelets to show a number bond. Lay them on a table. Put some beads in the first one and some beads in the second one. Put the total number of beads of the first two bracelets in the third one.
Week 35	Close your eyes and picture all of the equipment on the school playground. Open your eyes and draw the largest piece of equipment and the smallest piece of equipment.	Use washable paint and both of your hands to make a poster of the number 50. Stamp your hands five times. Count your fingers by 10s to 50.	Take out 10 cookies. Practice serving them on two plates. What are the amounts that can go on each plate? Tell number sentences to match your combinations.	Use chalk to draw a row of 10 circles on a sidewalk. Number them *1* to *10*. Use the number line to act out subtraction sentences such as *10 – 3*. Start on 10 and hop back 3 circles. Where did you land?
Week 36	Count the number of pillows in your home. Tell if that number is greater than or less than 10.	Draw 3 flowers with different numbers of petals. The stem represents 10. Each petal represents 1. Write the value of each flower in the middle. For example, a flower with 5 petals has a value of 15.	Write the numbers *0* to *9* in a column down the middle of a sheet of paper. Write the number *1* in front of each number. Say the new numbers aloud.	Write the numbers *0* to *9* on index cards. Have an adult say a number from 10 to 19. Use the index cards to build the number.

	Day 1	Day 2	Day 3	Day 4
Week 37	Find 15 rocks. Practice counting to 15. Then, group 10 rocks together. Count the group as 10 instead of starting from one. Which is quicker, starting from 1 or from 10?	How old are you? Use tally marks to show the numbers. Use objects from your home to build a set to show the number.	Ask an adult to use masking tape to make two ten frames on a rug. Use pennies to show the numbers 11 to 20 on the ten frames.	Find three examples of 3-D shapes in your home. Draw pictures of each object. Record the number of sides, edges, and faces.
Week 38	Roll two dice. Use cotton swabs as tally marks to show the number. Continue rolling and making tally marks until you have shown all of the numbers from 2 to 12.	Have an adult help you make a T-chart on construction paper. Label one side *Squares* and the other *Not Squares*. Glue pictures cut from magazines to the correct sides of the chart.	Do arm circles as you count from 0 to 25. Then, march in place as you count from 26 to 50.	Hold an apple in your hand. Find three objects in your home that are lighter than the apple. Then, find three objects that are heavier than the apple.
Week 39	Draw a monster. Make a pile of googly eyes. Label a die with *+1, +2, +3, −1, −2,* and *−3* on the sides. Roll the die. Add or take away that many eyes from the monster. How many eyes are left?	Put some dominoes in a bag. Take one out. Tell a number sentence to match the dots on the domino.	Stand in different locations around your home. Describe each location to a family member. For example, *I am behind the couch.*	Put a row of 10 stickers on a strip of paper. Cut off the ends of an envelope. Slip the strip partway inside the envelope. Tell how many are inside and how are outside of the envelope.
Week 40	Make a string of beads of the same color, shape, or kind. Add one bead to the sequence that is different. Challenge a family member to find the bead that does not belong.	Have an adult choose a number from 11 to 19. Have them tell you how many tens and ones in their number. What number is it?	Find pairs of objects in your home that are the same size.	Play a game of *I Spy* with a family member. Give clues that use location and physical attributes to help the other person guess the object. For example, *It is on top of the table. It is square. It is small.*

Count how many in each ten frame. Write the number.

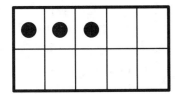   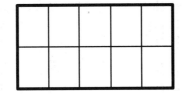   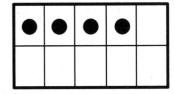

_____   _____   _____

Touch and count each number to 10.

1	2	3
4	5	6
7	8	9
	10	

Trace the number.

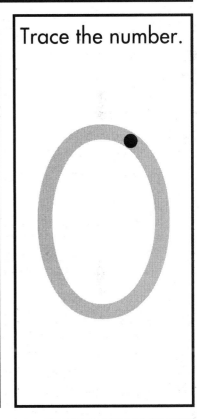

How many sides?

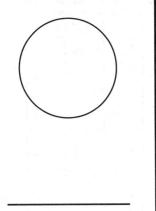

_____

Draw an object to make the picture true.

Circle the larger animal.

Circle the one that is long.

Circle the number that comes next.

3   4   5   6   7   [?]

9   8

Count how many backpacks.
Circle the number on the
number line.

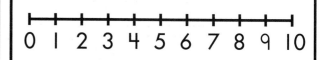
0 1 2 3 4 5 6 7 8 9 10

Circle the 2-D shapes.

 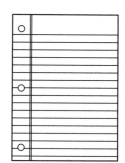

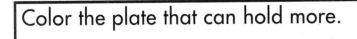

Color the plate that can hold more.

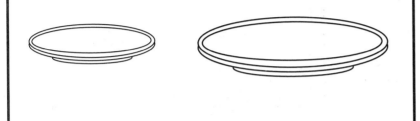

Match the sets to numbers.

2

4

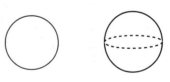

3

Amanda needs 5 eggs. Do you see 5 eggs?

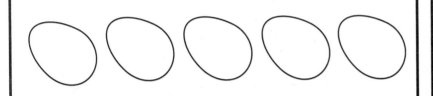

yes   **no**

Trace the number.

Color the cones purple.

Trace the shapes.

Trace the number.

2

David needs 4 balls. Do you see 4 balls?

yes   **no**

How many cubes long is the bear?

_____

Count and color to 1.

1	2	3	4	5	6	7	8	9	10
11	12	13	14	15	16	17	18	19	20
21	22	23	24	25	26	27	28	29	30
31	32	33	34	35	36	37	38	39	40
41	42	43	44	45	46	47	48	49	50
51	52	53	54	55	56	57	58	59	60
61	62	63	64	65	66	67	68	69	70
71	72	73	74	75	76	77	78	79	80
81	82	83	84	85	86	87	88	89	90
91	92	93	94	95	96	97	98	99	100

Circle the objects that go together.

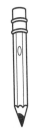   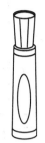 

Color the triangles blue.

Trace the number.

3

Glenn needs 4 bats. Are there 4 bats?

yes   no

Touch and count each number to 30.

1	2	3	4	5	6
7	8	9	10	11	12
13	14	15	16	17	18
19	20	21	22	23	24
25	26	27	28	29	30

How many?

_____

Draw a boy next to the girl.

Draw a lily pad beside the frog.

Circle the cat that is thin.

Trace the number.

Match the sets to numbers.

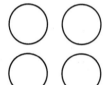

1

4

5

Count how many in each ten frame. Write the number.

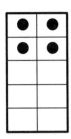 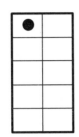 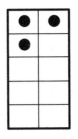

_____   _____   _____

Color the balloon with the longest string yellow. Color the one with the shortest string orange. Color the last balloon green.

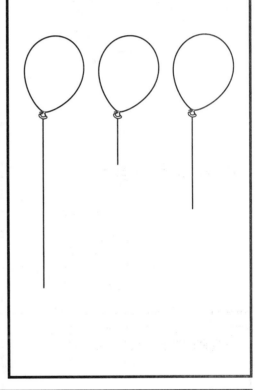

How many corners?

_____

Write the number that is one more.

5 _____

2 _____

8 _____

6 _____

Trace the number.

5

Is an  shorter than a ?

yes   **no**

Draw 2 triangles to add sails to the boat.

Trace the number.

6

Paula needs 8 carrots.
Are there 8 carrots?

yes   **no**

Count and color to 2.

1	2	3	4	5	6	7	8	9	10
11	12	13	14	15	16	17	18	19	20
21	22	23	24	25	26	27	28	29	30
31	32	33	34	35	36	37	38	39	40
41	42	43	44	45	46	47	48	49	50
51	52	53	54	55	56	57	58	59	60
61	62	63	64	65	66	67	68	69	70
71	72	73	74	75	76	77	78	79	80
81	82	83	84	85	86	87	88	89	90
91	92	93	94	95	96	97	98	99	100

How many?

   _____

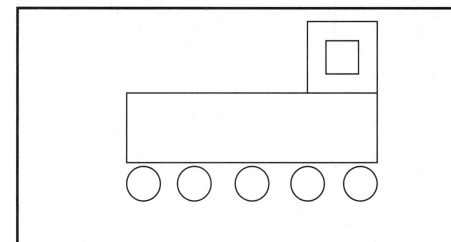

How many squares? _____

How many circles? _____

How many rectangles? _____

Trace the number.

Count how many.

_____

Draw an object to make the picture true.

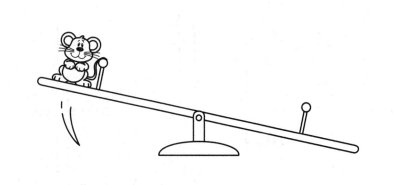

Write the number that is one more.

8 _____

9 _____

Color the jar that can hold more.

Trace the number.

Draw a balloon beside the cake.

Draw a spider below the web.

Count how many in each ten frame. Write the number.

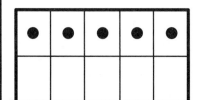

_____

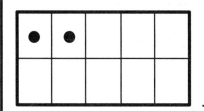

_____

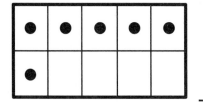

_____

Match the sets to numbers.

8

7

6

How many triangles are in the hexagon?

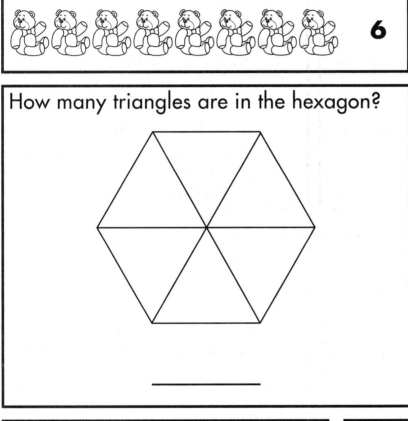

_____

Color the tree with 5 apples.

Circle the object that is heavy.

Trace the number.

Name _____

Color the correct number of objects.

5

Color the tower with more blocks.

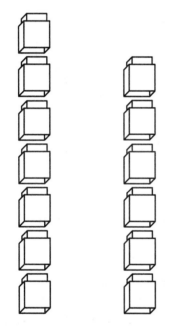

Draw yourself next to the trophy.

Trace the number.

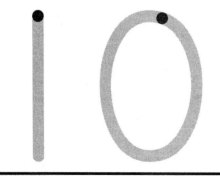

Count and color to 3.

1	2	3	4	5	6	7	8	9	10
11	12	13	14	15	16	17	18	19	20
21	22	23	24	25	26	27	28	29	30
31	32	33	34	35	36	37	38	39	40
41	42	43	44	45	46	47	48	49	50
51	52	53	54	55	56	57	58	59	60
61	62	63	64	65	66	67	68	69	70
71	72	73	74	75	76	77	78	79	80
81	82	83	84	85	86	87	88	89	90
91	92	93	94	95	96	97	98	99	100

Count the leaves. Circle the number on the number line.

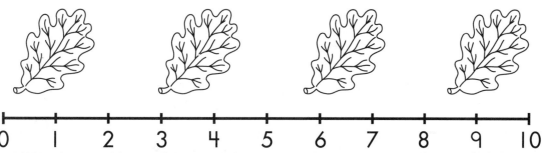

Color the heavy objects.

Find the number that is inside the square.

10

8

The number is

_____.

Draw a set to match the number.

3

Show the number on the ten frame.

10

Connect the dots to form a rectangle.

Circle the dog that is little.

Count how many in each ten frame. Write the number.

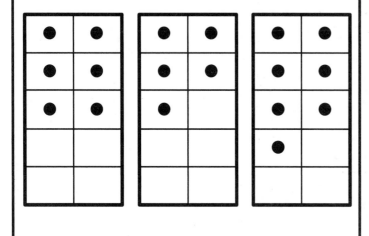

_____   _____   _____

Match the sets to numbers.

   **8**

Draw a set to match the number.

6

   **2**

          7

Color the correct number of objects.

8

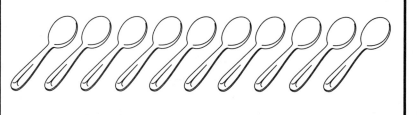

How many?

_____

_____

Color the circles.

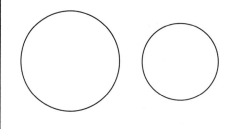

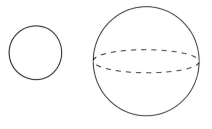

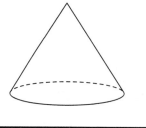

Start at 0. Connect the dots.

2

1   3

0   4

Circle the smaller bug.

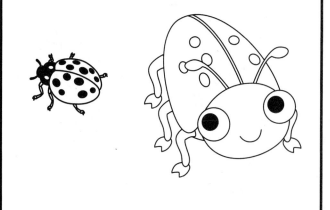

Match the sets to numbers.

5

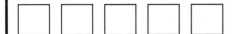

2

9

Count. Write each number.

_____ _____ _____

_____ _____ _____

_____ _____ _____

_____

Count how many in each ten frame. Write the number.

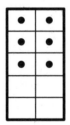 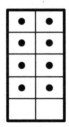 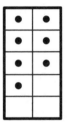

_____ _____ _____

Draw an **X** in front of the cup.

Count and color to 4.

1	2	3	4	5	6	7	8	9	10
11	12	13	14	15	16	17	18	19	20
21	22	23	24	25	26	27	28	29	30
31	32	33	34	35	36	37	38	39	40
41	42	43	44	45	46	47	48	49	50
51	52	53	54	55	56	57	58	59	60
61	62	63	64	65	66	67	68	69	70
71	72	73	74	75	76	77	78	79	80
81	82	83	84	85	86	87	88	89	90
91	92	93	94	95	96	97	98	99	100

Count on. Write the missing numbers.

3, _____ **,** _____ **,** _____

Count each set. Write the number.

 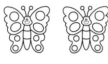

_____   _____   _____

Match the dice to numbers.

5

1

4

2

How many sides?

Color the longest rectangle red.
Color the shortest rectangle green.
Color the medium rectangle blue.

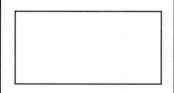

_____

Color the correct number of objects.

9

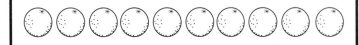

Help the bee find his way to the beehive by writing the missing numbers.

Color the container that can hold more.

Quart

Circle the student at the front of the line.

Match the sets to numbers.

2

10

7

Color the animals that belong in the ocean.

Count and color the sets.

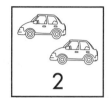 1
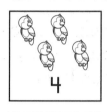 2

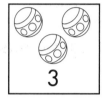 3
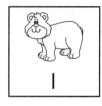 4

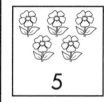 5
 6

 7
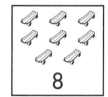 8

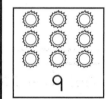 9
 10

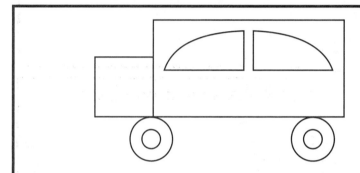

How many squares? _____

How many circles? _____

How many rectangles? _____

Draw an **X** on the box that does not show 9.

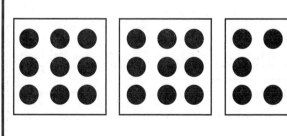

Color the rectangles blue.

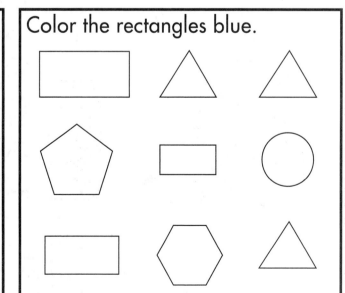

Draw the correct number of objects.

8

Circle the smooth object.

Put an **X** on the bee behind the hive.

How many?

_____

Count and color to 5.

1	2	3	4	5	6	7	8	9	10
11	12	13	14	15	16	17	18	19	20
21	22	23	24	25	26	27	28	29	30
31	32	33	34	35	36	37	38	39	40
41	42	43	44	45	46	47	48	49	50
51	52	53	54	55	56	57	58	59	60
61	62	63	64	65	66	67	68	69	70
71	72	73	74	75	76	77	78	79	80
81	82	83	84	85	86	87	88	89	90
91	92	93	94	95	96	97	98	99	100

Draw the correct number of objects.

5

How many?

_____

_____

circle

square

triangle

I have 3 sides.
What am I?

_____

Color the shortest pencil orange.
Color the longest pencil yellow.

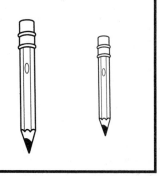

Color 8 cars.

Count on. Write the missing numbers.

6, _____ , _____ , _____

Count how many cats. Circle the number on the number line.

0 1 2 3 4 5 6 7 8 9 10

Color the shape that cannot roll.

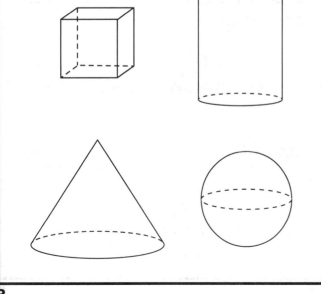

Color the shortest pencil blue.
Color the longest pencil red.

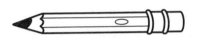

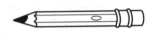

Match the sets to numbers.

   **9**

   **3**

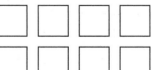   **10**

Match the sets to numbers.

⬡ ⬡ ⬡ ⬡ ⬡ ⬡ ⬡ ⬡   **9**

○ ○ ○ ○ ○ ○ ○ ○ ○   **5**

☐ ☐ ☐ ☐ ☐   **8**

Circle the shape that has 4 equal sides.

Count on. Write the missing numbers.

7, _____ , _____ , _____

Start with 0. Connect the dots.

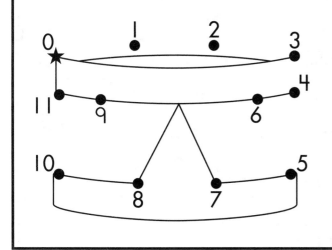

Put an **X** on the object that does not belong.

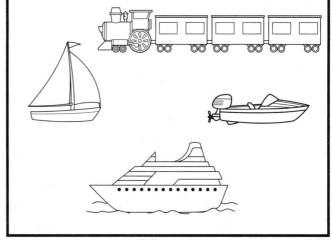

Color the flat shapes yellow.

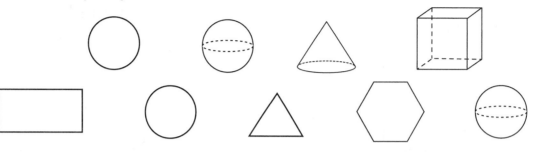

Write the number that is one more.

4 _____

0 _____

3 _____

1 _____

6 _____

2 _____

Draw a bear above the shelf.

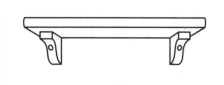

Color the bowl that can hold more.

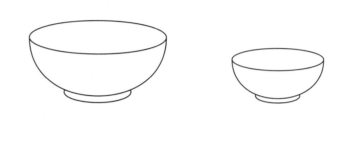

Count and color to 6.

1	2	3	4	5	6	7	8	9	10
11	12	13	14	15	16	17	18	19	20
21	22	23	24	25	26	27	28	29	30
31	32	33	34	35	36	37	38	39	40
41	42	43	44	45	46	47	48	49	50
51	52	53	54	55	56	57	58	59	60
61	62	63	64	65	66	67	68	69	70
71	72	73	74	75	76	77	78	79	80
81	82	83	84	85	86	87	88	89	90
91	92	93	94	95	96	97	98	99	100

40

Trace the circle. Draw more circles.

Look at the buttons. Circle the button that does not belong.

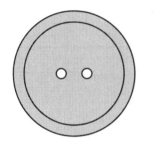
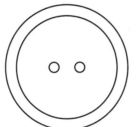

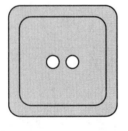
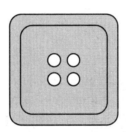

Write the number that is one more.

7 _____

1 _____

5 _____

8 _____

Color 4 circles.

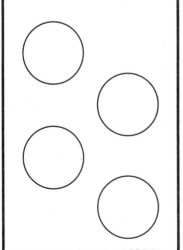

Circle the 3-D shape. Draw an **X** on the 2-D shape.

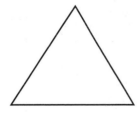
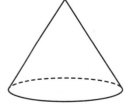

Color the correct number of objects.

5

Circle the heaviest cat.

How many sides?

_____

cone   cylinder   sphere

I am pointed at one end and flat at the other. What shape am I?

_____

Match the sets to numbers.

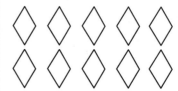   **9**

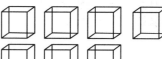   **7**

    10

Trace the shapes.

How many?

_____

Draw a set to match the number.

4

Circle the largest apple.

Write the number that is one more.

2 _____

0 _____

Write the number that is one less.

3 _____

4 _____

Draw the correct number of objects.

2

Circle the smallest object.

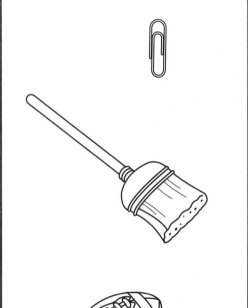

Trace the circle for a face. Then, add eyes, a nose, and a mouth.

Count and color to 7.

1	2	3	4	5	6	7	8	9	10
11	12	13	14	15	16	17	18	19	20
21	22	23	24	25	26	27	28	29	30
31	32	33	34	35	36	37	38	39	40
41	42	43	44	45	46	47	48	49	50
51	52	53	54	55	56	57	58	59	60
61	62	63	64	65	66	67	68	69	70
71	72	73	74	75	76	77	78	79	80
81	82	83	84	85	86	87	88	89	90
91	92	93	94	95	96	97	98	99	100

Write the missing numbers.

_____, **7,** _____

Circle the objects that are alike.

Here are 3 bugs.

Draw another set of 3.

Draw 4 triangles.

Draw the correct number of objects.

6

Circle the 3-D shape. Draw an **X** on the 2-D shape.

How many sides?

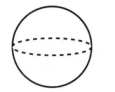

_____

Circle the largest rainbow.

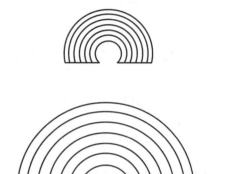

Tyrone needs 7 shirts. Are there 7 shirts?

yes   no

Color the correct number of blocks.

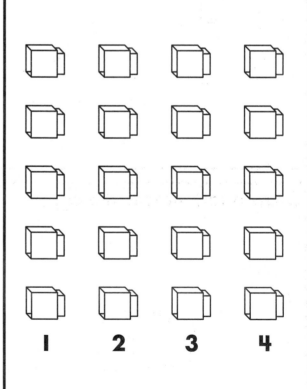

Trace the square. Draw a square.

Use different colors to sort the objects that are alike.

Color the correct number of objects.

3

Color the shapes that can roll.

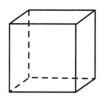

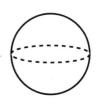

Draw a fork next to the egg.

How many?

_____

How many?

_____

How many faces?

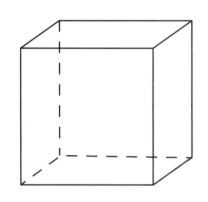

_____

Color 4.

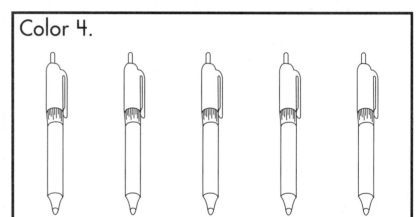

Which is the biggest?

Count and color to 8.

1	2	3	4	5	6	7	8	9	10
11	12	13	14	15	16	17	18	19	20
21	22	23	24	25	26	27	28	29	30
31	32	33	34	35	36	37	38	39	40
41	42	43	44	45	46	47	48	49	50
51	52	53	54	55	56	57	58	59	60
61	62	63	64	65	66	67	68	69	70
71	72	73	74	75	76	77	78	79	80
81	82	83	84	85	86	87	88	89	90
91	92	93	94	95	96	97	98	99	100

Draw a flower inside the circle.   Draw a feather beside the bird.

Stanley needs 10 frogs. Are there 10 frogs?

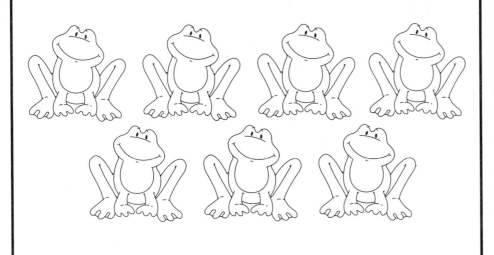

yes   **no**

Color the correct number of objects.

8

Circle the objects that are alike.

Color the cubes blue.

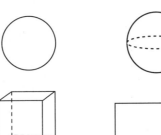

Draw 2 circles.

---

cube   cylinder   sphere

I am the shape of a can of soup.

What shape am I?

_____

Draw the correct number of objects.

7

Use two colors to show different ways to make 5.

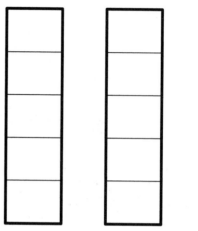

Color the tallest chair green.
Color the shortest chair red.

Draw a shape with 3 sides.

Draw the correct number of objects.

9

Here are 9 blocks.

Draw another set of 9.

Draw a worm below the dirt.

Draw a house. Use one rectangle and one triangle.

Trace the triangle. Draw more triangles.

Write the number that is one more.

5 _____

9 _____

2 _____

4 _____

Color the correct number of objects.

6

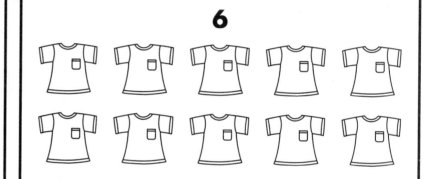

Color the pitcher that can hold the most milk.

Count and color to 9.

1	2	3	4	5	6	7	8	9	10
11	12	13	14	15	16	17	18	19	20
21	22	23	24	25	26	27	28	29	30
31	32	33	34	35	36	37	38	39	40
41	42	43	44	45	46	47	48	49	50
51	52	53	54	55	56	57	58	59	60
61	62	63	64	65	66	67	68	69	70
71	72	73	74	75	76	77	78	79	80
81	82	83	84	85	86	87	88	89	90
91	92	93	94	95	96	97	98	99	100

Color more than 1 apple.

Use the pattern blocks shown to cover the hexagon. Use different colors to show your work.

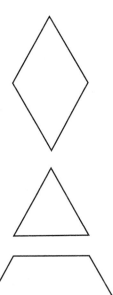 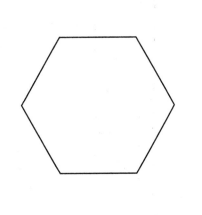

Circle the cup with more.

Trace the number.

Count. Write each number.

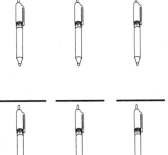

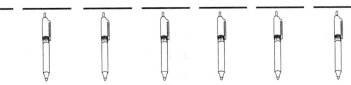

Circle the object that weighs more.

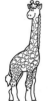

How many?

_____

Trace the number.

Circle the ten frame that shows 11.

Count the dots. Write a number that is more.

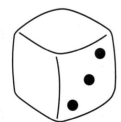

_____

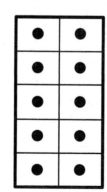

Write in the missing 10s.

1	2	3	4	5	6	7	8	9	
11	12	13	14	15	16	17	18	19	
21	22	23	24	25	26	27	28	29	

Color the balloon with the greater number.

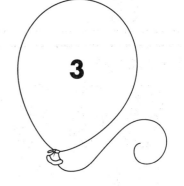

3

4

Circle the tallest pair of shoes.

Trace the number.

1 3

Match the sets to numbers.

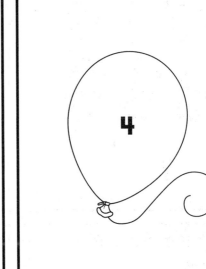

13

11

10

Circle the set of blocks that will make the picture true.

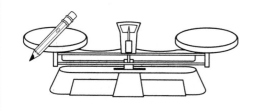 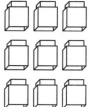

How many?

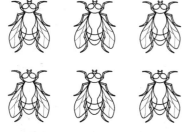

_____

Which ten frame has the most? Color it yellow.

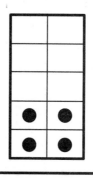 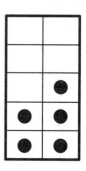

Trace the number.

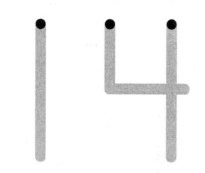

Count and color to 10.

1	2	3	4	5	6	7	8	9	10
11	12	13	14	15	16	17	18	19	20
21	22	23	24	25	26	27	28	29	30
31	32	33	34	35	36	37	38	39	40
41	42	43	44	45	46	47	48	49	50
51	52	53	54	55	56	57	58	59	60
61	62	63	64	65	66	67	68	69	70
71	72	73	74	75	76	77	78	79	80
81	82	83	84	85	86	87	88	89	90
91	92	93	94	95	96	97	98	99	100

Draw an **X** 14 times.

How many sides does each shape have?

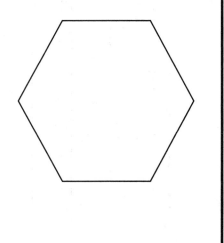

_____   _____

An 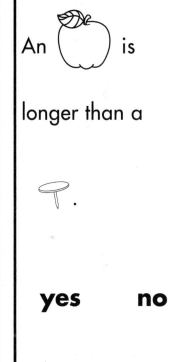 is

longer than a

.

yes   **no**

Circle the nail that is taller.

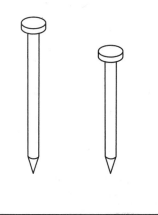

Color the shape with the least number of sides.

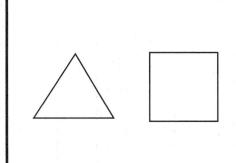

Touch and count each number to 10.

1	2	3	4	5
6	7	8	9	10
11	12	13	14	15

Which object is there more of?

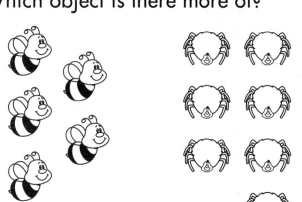

_____

Draw a set with 1 more.

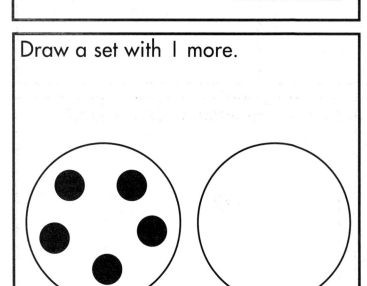

Draw 6 balls in each basket.

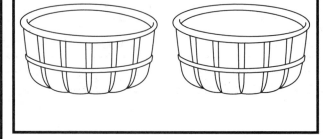

Match the sets to numbers.

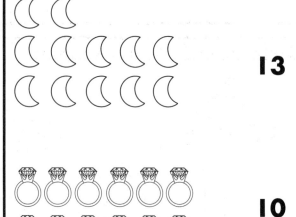

12

13

10

Match the sets to numbers.

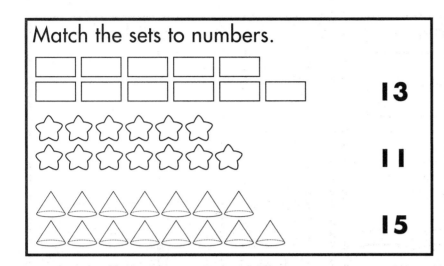

13

11

15

Draw the correct number of objects.

15

Draw a chair for each doll.

How many chairs? _____

Circle the child that is shortest.

Circle the number that is least.

10   7

9   8

Color the objects that are light.

How many?

_____ _

Draw pencils to match the number.

13

Count the dots. Write a number that is more.

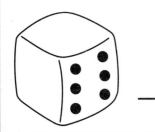

_____

Count and color to 11.

1	2	3	4	5	6	7	8	9	10
11	12	13	14	15	16	17	18	19	20
21	22	23	24	25	26	27	28	29	30
31	32	33	34	35	36	37	38	39	40
41	42	43	44	45	46	47	48	49	50
51	52	53	54	55	56	57	58	59	60
61	62	63	64	65	66	67	68	69	70
71	72	73	74	75	76	77	78	79	80
81	82	83	84	85	86	87	88	89	90
91	92	93	94	95	96	97	98	99	100

60

Color the triangles yellow. Color the cones red.

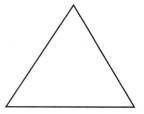 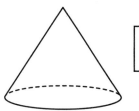

Use different colors to sort the objects that are alike.

Color the box with the number that is more.

```
8
```

```
7
```

How many?

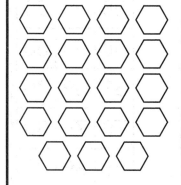

17   19   18

Draw lines to match each dog with a bone.

Is there an equal number of dogs and bones?

yes   no

Count and write the missing numbers.

_____ , _____ , _____ , 18

Count how many. Write the number. Color the group of birds that is greater.

_____   _____

Write the missing number.

10   11

13   14

Look at the numbers. Complete the sentence.

| 3 | 5 |

_____ is less than _____.

How many are the same shape?

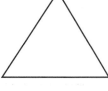

 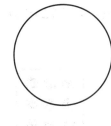

_____

Are the sets equal? If yes, circle the **=**. If no, draw an **X** on the **=**.

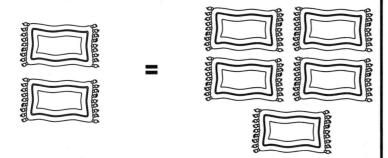

Color the correct number of blocks.

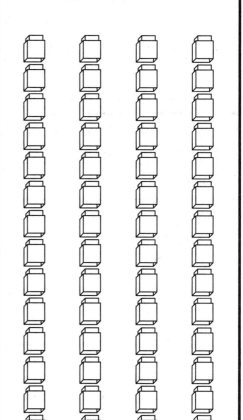

10   11   12   13

Count how many. Write the number. Circle the set that is greater.

_____   _____

Count. How many dots in all?

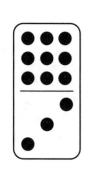
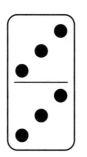

_____

Circle the object that is shortest.

Draw a set with one less.

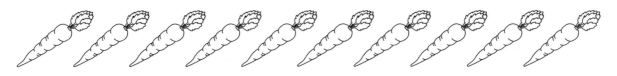

Color the sailboat with 12 dark stripes.

Count on. Write the missing numbers.

12, _____ , _____ , _____

Circle the object that is soft.

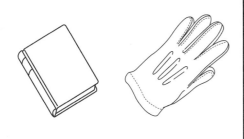

Count and color to 12.

1	2	3	4	5	6	7	8	9	10
11	12	13	14	15	16	17	18	19	20
21	22	23	24	25	26	27	28	29	30
31	32	33	34	35	36	37	38	39	40
41	42	43	44	45	46	47	48	49	50
51	52	53	54	55	56	57	58	59	60
61	62	63	64	65	66	67	68	69	70
71	72	73	74	75	76	77	78	79	80
81	82	83	84	85	86	87	88	89	90
91	92	93	94	95	96	97	98	99	100

Color the same amount in each set.

Circle the set that is greater.

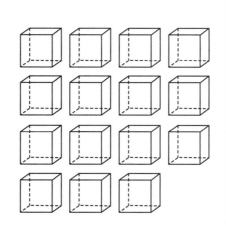

Circle the one that weighs less.

How many?

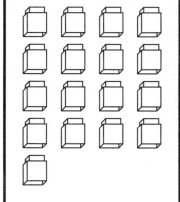

_____

Draw 10 suns.

Circle the greater number.

8   5

Count the dots. Write a number that is more.

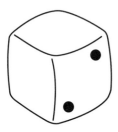

_____

Circle the pair of ten frames that show 12.

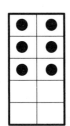 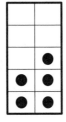

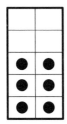 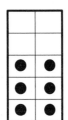

Mary needs 17 books. Are there 17 books?

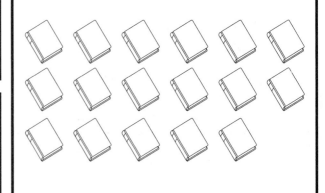

yes   no

Color the shape with the least number of sides yellow.

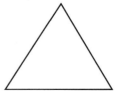

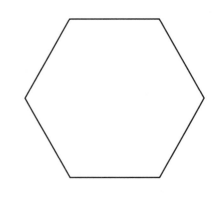

Count how many ants. Circle the number on the number line.

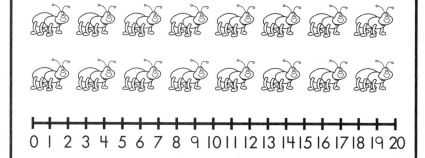

Color the die with the most dots.

Draw a set that is equal.

Color the banana with the smallest number.

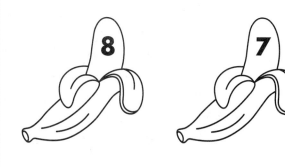

Fill in the missing number.

How many cars long is the train?

_____

How many?

○ ○ ○ ○
○ ○ ○ ○
○ ○ ○ ○
○ ○ ○ ○
○ ○ ○

_____

Count to 11. Draw 11 circles.

Are the sets equal? If yes, circle the **=**. If no, draw an **X** on the **=**.

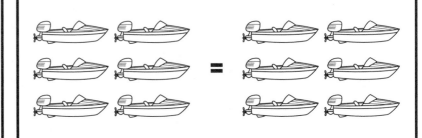

Count and color to 13.

1	2	3	4	5	6	7	8	9	10
11	12	13	14	15	16	17	18	19	20
21	22	23	24	25	26	27	28	29	30
31	32	33	34	35	36	37	38	39	40
41	42	43	44	45	46	47	48	49	50
51	52	53	54	55	56	57	58	59	60
61	62	63	64	65	66	67	68	69	70
71	72	73	74	75	76	77	78	79	80
81	82	83	84	85	86	87	88	89	90
91	92	93	94	95	96	97	98	99	100

Circle the train with the least number of cars.

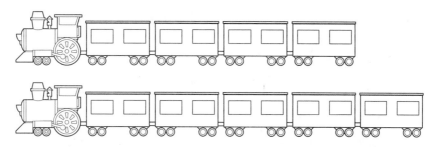

Color the flower with the biggest number.

Color the triangles blue.

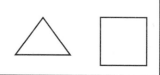

Color the set that shows more.

Color the box with the number that is more.

10   6

Color the balloon with the greater number.

Draw two equal sets of 7.

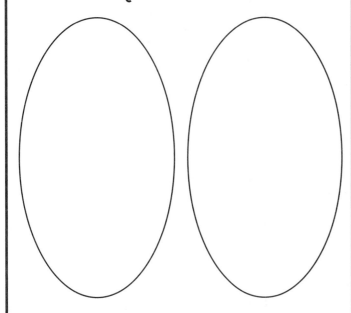

Color the shape with the most number of sides.

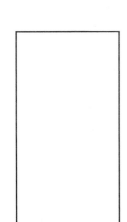
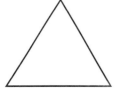

Compare the ten frames. Color the one that has the most.

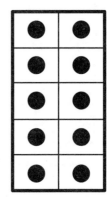 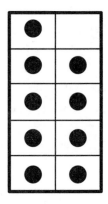

How many more blocks longer is the first fork?

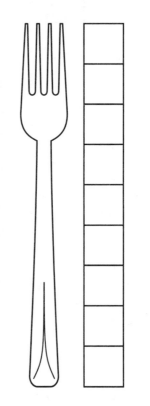

_____ **blocks**

Count the bells. Write the number. Color the group of bells that is greater.

_____

_____

Use pattern blocks to draw a flower.

Put an **X** on the object that does not belong.

Circle the object that will make the picture true.

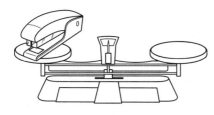

Circle the number that is one more than 5.

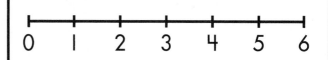

0   1   2   3   4   5   6

Circle the shapes that could not make the rectangle.

 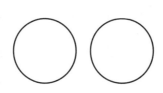 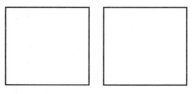

Color the same amount of squares in each set.

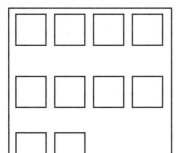

Circle the number that is one less than 7.

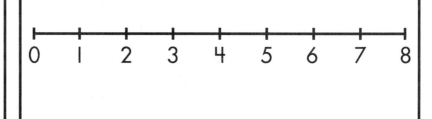

Count and color to 14.

1	2	3	4	5	6	7	8	9	10
11	12	13	14	15	16	17	18	19	20
21	22	23	24	25	26	27	28	29	30
31	32	33	34	35	36	37	38	39	40
41	42	43	44	45	46	47	48	49	50
51	52	53	54	55	56	57	58	59	60
61	62	63	64	65	66	67	68	69	70
71	72	73	74	75	76	77	78	79	80
81	82	83	84	85	86	87	88	89	90
91	92	93	94	95	96	97	98	99	100

Use < or > to compare.

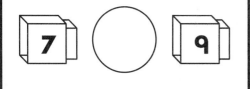

Color 3 circles red and 4 circles orange.

How many did you color altogether? _____

Touch and count each number. Color the 10s.

1	2	3	4	5	6
7	8	9	10	11	12
13	14	15	16	17	18
19	20	21	22	23	24
25	26	27	28	29	30

rectangle

square

Name the shapes.

_____

_____

Use the numbers to complete the sentence.

7	9

_____ is less

than _____.

Draw a set that is equal.

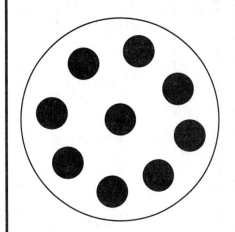 =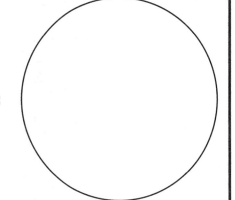

Write the number that is one more.

18, _____

19, _____

Draw a set with one less.

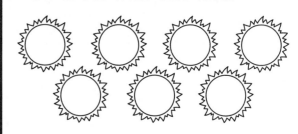

Color the two shapes with an equal number of sides.

Color 3 hearts red and 2 hearts blue. Then, write the total number of hearts.

_____

Color the box with the number that is less.

10	8

Color the hole the shape would fit through.

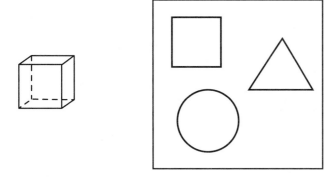

Start at 0. Connect the dots.

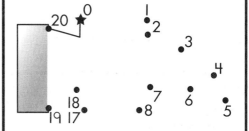

I have 1 apple. How many more do I need to make 5? Draw them.

_____

Color the balloon with the greater number.

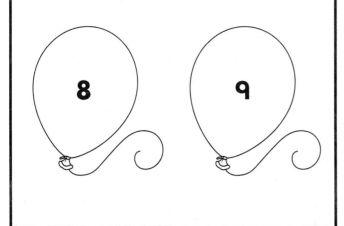

Color the smallest number red.

Color 15 snails.

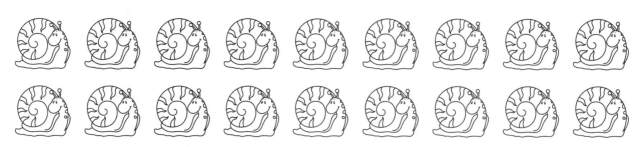

Color the shape that is the same.

Color the two dice that make 7.

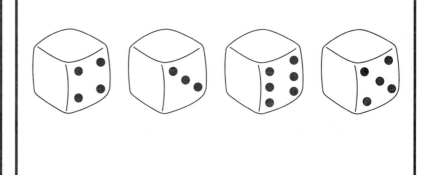

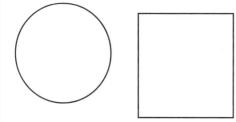

Count and color to 15.

1	2	3	4	5	6	7	8	9	10
11	12	13	14	15	16	17	18	19	20
21	22	23	24	25	26	27	28	29	30
31	32	33	34	35	36	37	38	39	40
41	42	43	44	45	46	47	48	49	50
51	52	53	54	55	56	57	58	59	60
61	62	63	64	65	66	67	68	69	70
71	72	73	74	75	76	77	78	79	80
81	82	83	84	85	86	87	88	89	90
91	92	93	94	95	96	97	98	99	100

Count the dots. Write a number that is less.

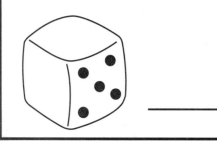 _____

Name _____   **Week 16, Day 1**

How many?

_____   _____

Circle the bowl that has more gumdrops.

How many?

_____

How many?

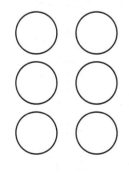

_____

Circle the number that comes next.

0   1   2   3   4   ?

3   5

Count how many dots. Write the number.

_____

Count. Write each number.

_____   _____   _____   _____   _____

_____   _____   _____   _____   _____

Start at 0. Connect the dots.

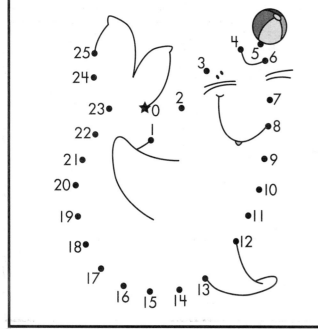

25
24
23
22
21
20
19
18
17
16 15 14 13
12
11
10
9
8
7
6
5
4
3
2
0
1

How many?

_____

Circle the child who is the tallest.

How many?

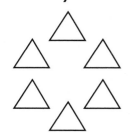 

_____   _____

Count the scoops. Draw scoops to show 3 more.

Match the sets to numbers.

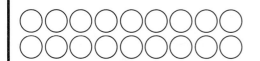

15

20

18

How many?

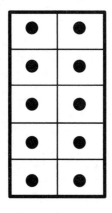

_____

Count. How many dots in all?

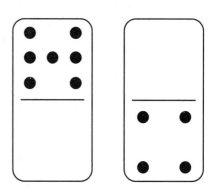

_____

Circle the pair of ten frames that shows 14.

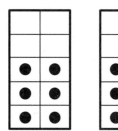 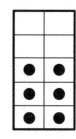 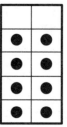

Circle the worm that is longer.

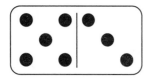

Draw the correct number of objects.

10

Count how many.

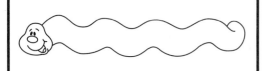

_____

Count and color to 16.

1	2	3	4	5	6	7	8	9	10
11	12	13	14	15	16	17	18	19	20
21	22	23	24	25	26	27	28	29	30
31	32	33	34	35	36	37	38	39	40
41	42	43	44	45	46	47	48	49	50
51	52	53	54	55	56	57	58	59	60
61	62	63	64	65	66	67	68	69	70
71	72	73	74	75	76	77	78	79	80
81	82	83	84	85	86	87	88	89	90
91	92	93	94	95	96	97	98	99	100

Write the number that is one more.

4 _____   3 _____   2 _____

5 _____   1 _____   6 _____

Color the circles.

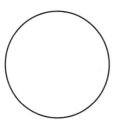 

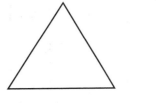

Circle the set that is greater.

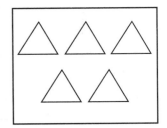

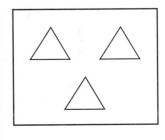

Circle the one that is the lightest.

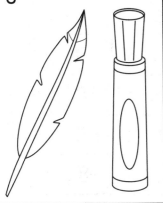

Color the objects that are alike.

Color the two bubbles that make 2.

Draw a sun above the cloud

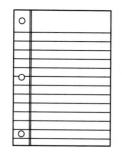

Draw a pencil in front of the paper.

Circle the animals that can fly.

Connect the dots to make a triangle.

Circle the set that is less.

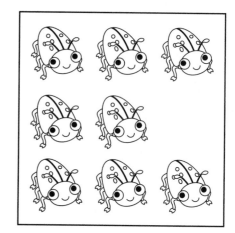

Draw a line to complete the shape.

How many sides does it have? _____

Here are 7 birds.

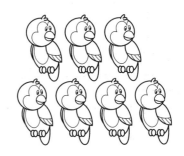

Draw another set of 7.

Circle the objects that are alike.

Draw a shark below the water.

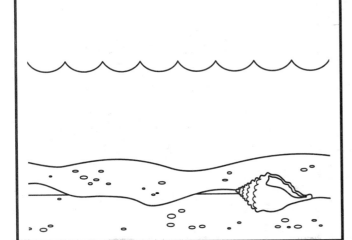

Draw a set that is one more.

Circle the set that is less.

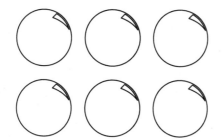

Draw a 3-D shape.

Draw a 2-D shape.

Circle the object that is the hardest.

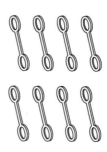
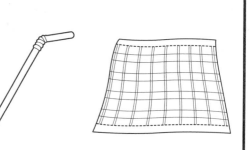

Count and color to 17.

1	2	3	4	5	6	7	8	9	10
11	12	13	14	15	16	17	18	19	20
21	22	23	24	25	26	27	28	29	30
31	32	33	34	35	36	37	38	39	40
41	42	43	44	45	46	47	48	49	50
51	52	53	54	55	56	57	58	59	60
61	62	63	64	65	66	67	68	69	70
71	72	73	74	75	76	77	78	79	80
81	82	83	84	85	86	87	88	89	90
91	92	93	94	95	96	97	98	99	100

Color the smallest number purple.

Circle the 3-D shapes.

Color the longest snake brown.
Color the shortest snake red.

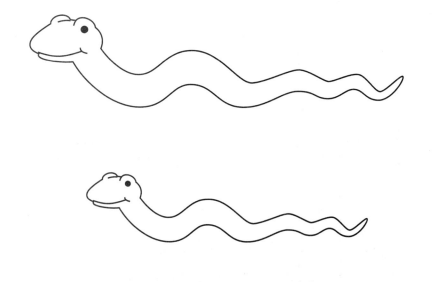

Color the box
with the number
that is less.

6

4

Color the two
triangles that
make 3.

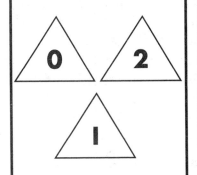

Here are 6 puppies.

Draw another set of 6.

Name _____

Color the shortest can yellow.
Color the tallest can pink.

Cindy needs 9 sheets of paper. Are there 9 sheets of paper?

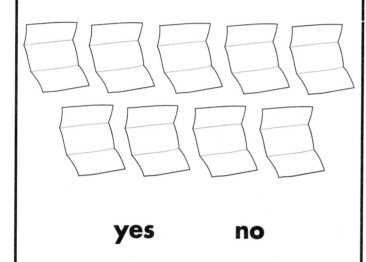

yes   **no**

Draw 5 objects.

cone   cube   cylinder

I have six faces. What shape am I?

_____

Circle the tower with the most blocks.

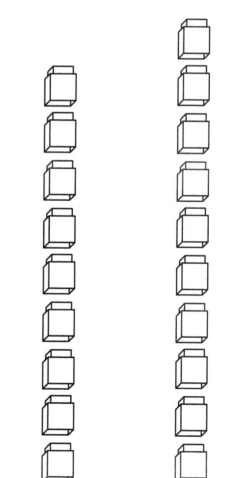

Draw a dog behind the fence.

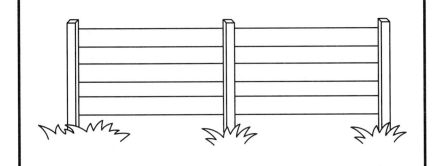

Use **<**, **>**, or **=** to compare.

6 ⬡ 5

3 ⬡ 3

4 ⬡ 8

Circle the big gum balls. Draw an **X** on the small gum balls.

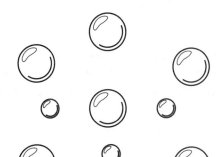

How many big gum balls? _____

How many small gum balls? _____

Which do you have the most of? _____

Write the number that is one more.

6 _____

4 _____

Put an **X** on the object that does not belong.

Use **<** or **>** to compare.

 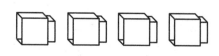

Here are 8 lemons.

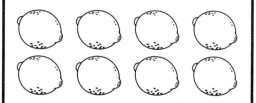

Draw another set of 8.

Circle the set of blocks that will make the picture true.

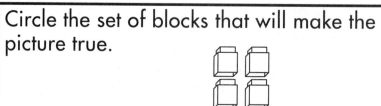

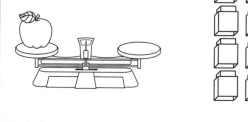

Draw a person above the square.

Count and color to 18.

1	2	3	4	5	6	7	8	9	10
11	12	13	14	15	16	17	18	19	20
21	22	23	24	25	26	27	28	29	30
31	32	33	34	35	36	37	38	39	40
41	42	43	44	45	46	47	48	49	50
51	52	53	54	55	56	57	58	59	60
61	62	63	64	65	66	67	68	69	70
71	72	73	74	75	76	77	78	79	80
81	82	83	84	85	86	87	88	89	90
91	92	93	94	95	96	97	98	99	100

Circle the 2-D shapes.

How many?

Circle the child
that is taller.

_____

How many
corners?

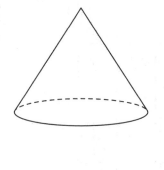

_____

How many big balloons are there? _____

How many small balloons are there? _____

Name _____

A hexagon has more sides than a square.

yes   **no**

Touch and count each number to 20.

1	2	3	4
5	6	7	8
9	10	11	12
13	14	15	16
17	18	19	20

Color 2 spiders brown and 4 spiders black. How many did you color altogether?

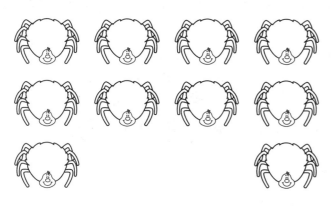

_____

Match the sets to numbers.

△ △ △ △ △
△ △ △ △ △   **5**

○ ○ ○ ○ ○   **10**

☐ ☐ ☐ ☐ ☐
☐ ☐ ☐ ☐   **9**

Circle the 3-D shapes.

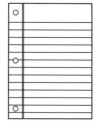

Color the same amount in each set.

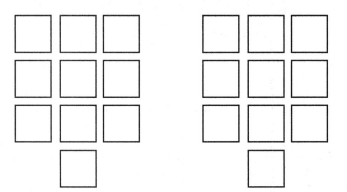

Complete the sentences with a picture or word.

A cylinder can _____.

A _____ cannot.

Match each flower to a pot.

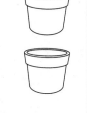

Is there an equal amount of each?

yes   **no**

Circle the net that has more.

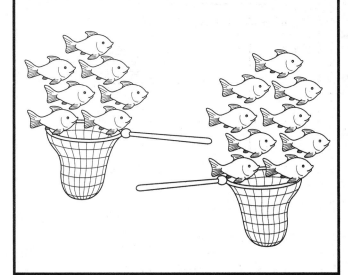

Count the dots. Write the number.

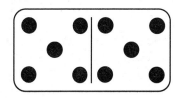

_____

How many?

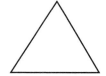 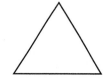   _____

Color the set that has more.

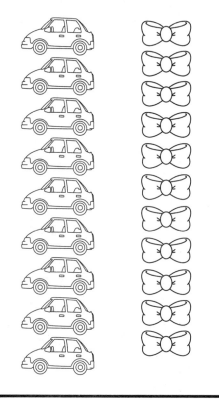

This shape has _____ sides

and _____ corners.

Draw a person beside the square.

Count and color to 19.

1	2	3	4	5	6	7	8	9	10
11	12	13	14	15	16	17	18	19	20
21	22	23	24	25	26	27	28	29	30
31	32	33	34	35	36	37	38	39	40
41	42	43	44	45	46	47	48	49	50
51	52	53	54	55	56	57	58	59	60
61	62	63	64	65	66	67	68	69	70
71	72	73	74	75	76	77	78	79	80
81	82	83	84	85	86	87	88	89	90
91	92	93	94	95	96	97	98	99	100

Draw an object to make the picture true.

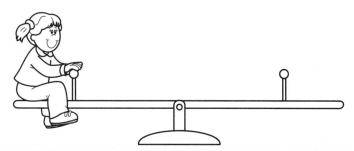

Use different colors to sort the objects that are alike.

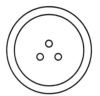 

 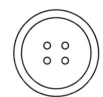 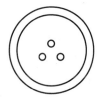

How many?

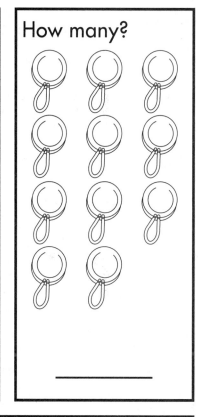

_____

Write a number to make the comparison true.

_____ > **6**

Count how many. Write the number.

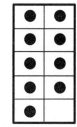   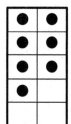   [number frame]

_____   _____   _____

Draw 11 tally marks.

How many white bears do you see? _____

Which set has the most?

gray   **white**

Color the pail with the most shells yellow.

Draw a set with one more.

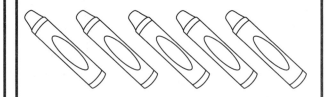

Draw more dots to make 10.

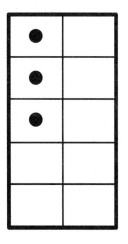

Draw 8 hearts.

How many blocks tall is the tower?

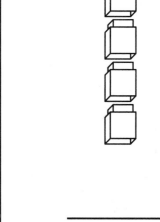

Use two colors to show different ways to make 10.

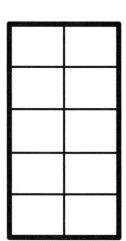 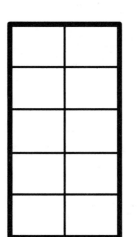

_____

Use the numbers to make each comparison true.

5   4

_____ **<** _____

_____ **>** _____

Color the shape with the most sides red.

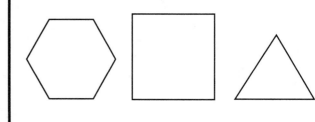

Count how many dots on each domino.

_____   _____   _____

How many spheres?

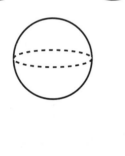

_____

Circle the set of blocks that will make the picture true.

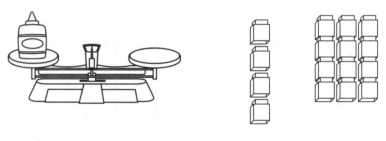

A 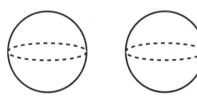 is longer

than a 🐞 .

yes   **no**

Count and color to 20.

1	2	3	4	5	6	7	8	9	10
11	12	13	14	15	16	17	18	19	20
21	22	23	24	25	26	27	28	29	30
31	32	33	34	35	36	37	38	39	40
41	42	43	44	45	46	47	48	49	50
51	52	53	54	55	56	57	58	59	60
61	62	63	64	65	66	67	68	69	70
71	72	73	74	75	76	77	78	79	80
81	82	83	84	85	86	87	88	89	90
91	92	93	94	95	96	97	98	99	100

How long?

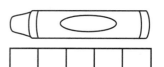

_____ **blocks**   _____ **blocks**

Use shapes to draw a map of your room.

Count by 2s.
Color the numbers you say green.

1	2	3	4
5	6	7	8
9	10	11	12
13	14	15	16
17	18	19	20

Use < or > to compare.

5 ◯ **7**

Color the largest set red. Color the smallest set blue.

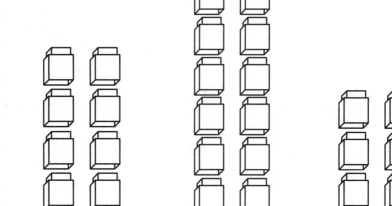

Use < or > to compare.

Draw some red circles and some green circles. How many circles did you draw altogether?

_____ + _____ = _____

Circle the longest train.

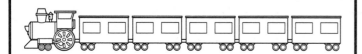

Draw things that are triangles. Draw things that are not triangles.

Triangles	Not Triangles

Draw scoops of ice cream to match the number.

10

Complete the sentences with a picture or word.

A _____ is a flat shape. A

_____ is a solid shape.

Count how many. Write the number. Circle the set with the most.

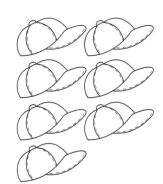 

_____   _____

Use two colors to show different ways to make 10.

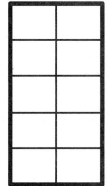

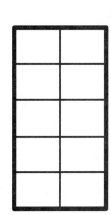

Color the largest number red.

3 5 2

I caught 10 fireflies. Some are in a jar. Some are flying around. Draw a picture to match the story.

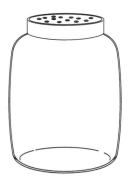

Use **<** or **>** to compare.

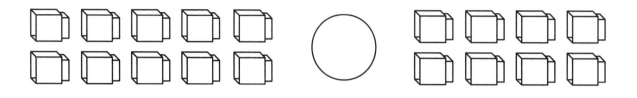

Circle the tower with the most blocks.

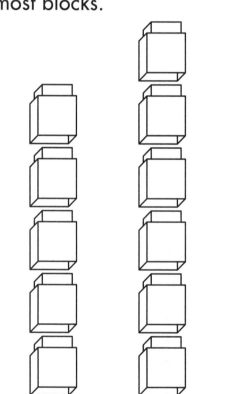

How many?

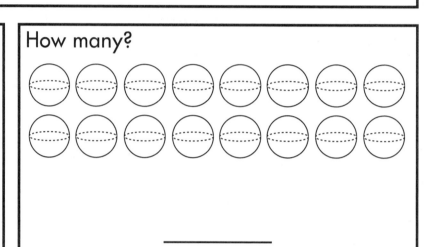

_____

Count and color to 21.

1	2	3	4	5	6	7	8	9	10
11	12	13	14	15	16	17	18	19	20
21	22	23	24	25	26	27	28	29	30
31	32	33	34	35	36	37	38	39	40
41	42	43	44	45	46	47	48	49	50
51	52	53	54	55	56	57	58	59	60
61	62	63	64	65	66	67	68	69	70
71	72	73	74	75	76	77	78	79	80
81	82	83	84	85	86	87	88	89	90
91	92	93	94	95	96	97	98	99	100

What number comes next?

15, _____

Color the pig with the number 16 on it.

Count the petals. Write how many.

_____

Draw 17 circles.

Color the fruit that has the larger number.

Circle the correct answers.

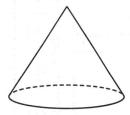

A cone is flat.   **yes**   **no**

A cone can roll.   **yes**   **no**

How many faces?

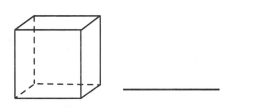

_____

Match the sets to numbers.

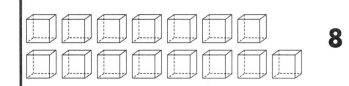

15

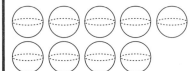

9

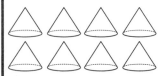

8

Count by 2s. Color the numbers you say yellow.

1	2	3	4	5
6	7	8	9	10
11	12	13	14	15
16	17	18	19	20
21	22	23	24	25
26	27	28	29	30

Use **<**, **>**, or **=** to compare.

4 4

Color the shape that is the same.

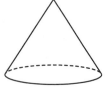

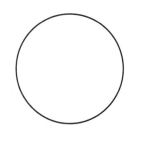

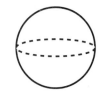

Use the numbers to make each comparison true.

| 4 | 5 | 4 |

_____ = _____

_____ > _____

Count. Write each number.

_____ _____ _____

_____ _____ _____

_____ _____ _____

_____ _____ _____

_____ _____ _____

_____ _____ _____

Color the correct number of objects.

16

Write the missing numbers.

17, _____ , _____

Name and draw a sphere in your classroom.

_____

Circle the correct number to show how many.

 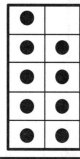

19   18

Draw a set with less.

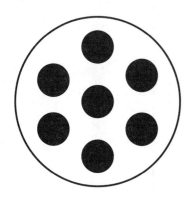

Connect the dots to make a rectangle.

Count and color to 22.

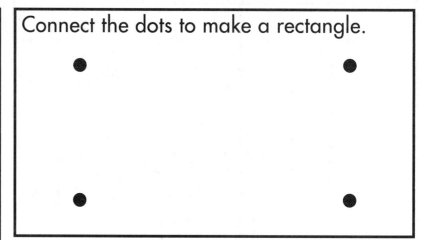

1	2	3	4	5	6	7	8	9	10
11	12	13	14	15	16	17	18	19	20
21	22	23	24	25	26	27	28	29	30
31	32	33	34	35	36	37	38	39	40
41	42	43	44	45	46	47	48	49	50
51	52	53	54	55	56	57	58	59	60
61	62	63	64	65	66	67	68	69	70
71	72	73	74	75	76	77	78	79	80
81	82	83	84	85	86	87	88	89	90
91	92	93	94	95	96	97	98	99	100

How many? _____

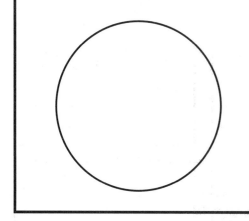

Trace the square. Draw more squares.

Trace the number. Count the objects.

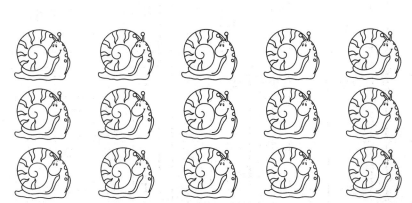

Color less than 3 circles.

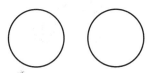
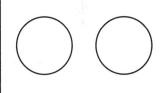

A cube has six faces.

yes

no

How many balls are in the net? _____

How many balls are outside the net? _____

How many balls altogether? _____

_____ + _____ = _____

Connect the dots to make a circle.

How many?

_____

Write the missing part.

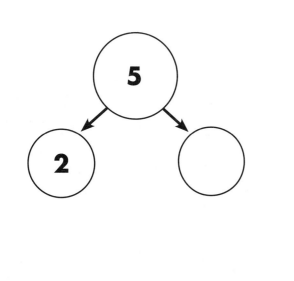

I have 10 gumballs. Some are in the gumball machine. Some fell out. Draw a picture to tell the story.

Color the shape with 1 face.

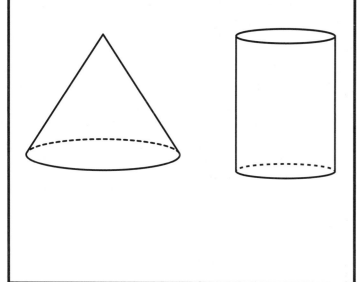

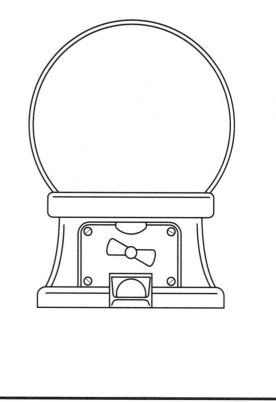

Color the correct number of blocks.

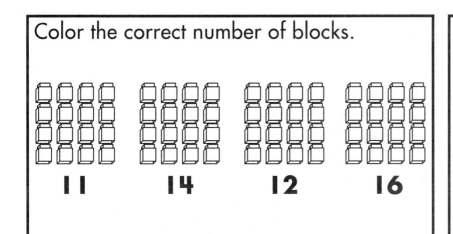

11   14   12   16

Use the numbers to make each comparison true.

5   8

_____ > _____

_____ < _____

Draw more tally marks to make 10.

|

Match the shapes to real-world objects.

paint can

tissue box

ice-cream cone

Write a word or draw a picture to make the sentence true.

A cube cannot roll like

a _____.

Circle the two numbers that are equal.

7   9   6   9   5   8

Write the missing parts.

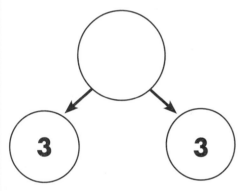

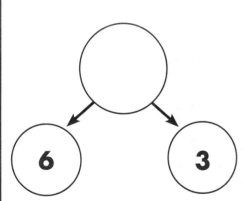

Draw legs to give the bug 10 legs in all.

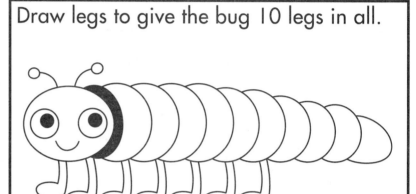

Circle the small shapes.
Color the big shapes.

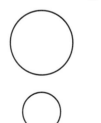

Count and color to 23.

1	2	3	4	5	6	7	8	9	10
11	12	13	14	15	16	17	18	19	20
21	22	23	24	25	26	27	28	29	30
31	32	33	34	35	36	37	38	39	40
41	42	43	44	45	46	47	48	49	50
51	52	53	54	55	56	57	58	59	60
61	62	63	64	65	66	67	68	69	70
71	72	73	74	75	76	77	78	79	80
81	82	83	84	85	86	87	88	89	90
91	92	93	94	95	96	97	98	99	100

Circle the triangle that is different.

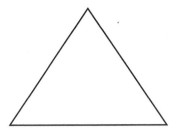 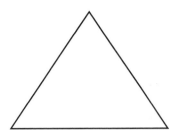 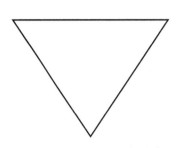

Write a number sentence.

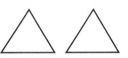

_____ **+** _____ **=** _____

Draw one more shoe. How many shoes altogether?

_____

square

triangle

A _____
has more
sides than a
_____ .

Match the sets to numbers.

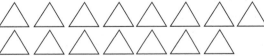

17

11

15

A cylinder has 2 faces.

yes   **no**

Connect the dots to make a square.

●   ●

●   ●

Color two dice that make 8.

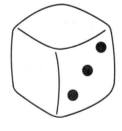 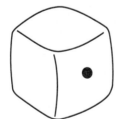

Circle a group of 10.

Complete the number sentences.

12 = 10 + _____

_____ + 10 = 12

Count. Write each number.

_____   _____   _____

_____   _____   _____

_____   _____   _____

_____   _____   _____

_____   _____   _____

Write two numbers to make the statement true. Draw a picture to show how you know.

_____ **is less than** _____ .

What shape is it?

_____

Write a number sentence.

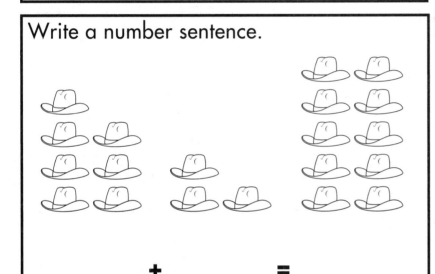

_____ **+** _____ **=** _____

Draw things that are circles. Draw things that are not a circles.

Circles	**Not Circles**

Use the ten frames to show 19.

Color 7 circles blue and 8 circles green. How many did you color altogether?

_____

Color the same amount in each set.

Count by 10s. Color the numbers you say.

1	2	3	4	5	6	7	8	9	10
11	12	13	14	15	16	17	18	19	20
21	22	23	24	25	26	27	28	29	30

A cone has more faces than a cylinder.

yes   **no**

Count and color to 24.

1	2	3	4	5	6	7	8	9	10
11	12	13	14	15	16	17	18	19	20
21	22	23	24	25	26	27	28	29	30
31	32	33	34	35	36	37	38	39	40
41	42	43	44	45	46	47	48	49	50
51	52	53	54	55	56	57	58	59	60
61	62	63	64	65	66	67	68	69	70
71	72	73	74	75	76	77	78	79	80
81	82	83	84	85	86	87	88	89	90
91	92	93	94	95	96	97	98	99	100

Circle the shapes you need to make the bigger shape.

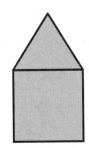   

Write a number sentence.

_____ + _____ = _____

Color the correct number of blocks.

18

Name and draw a 3-D object.

_____

Write a number sentence to tell about the picture.

_____ + _____ = _____

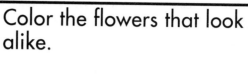

A _____ has _____ corners and _____ faces.

Draw 4 squares.

Color the flowers that look alike.

How many crayons?

_____

Match the sets to numbers.

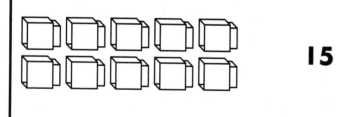   15

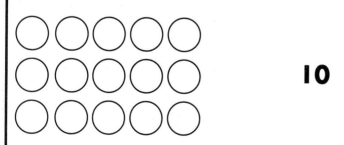   10

Circle the bear that is dark.

Complete the tree with a circle.

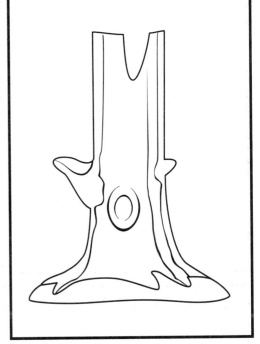

Draw real-world objects that match each 2-D shape.

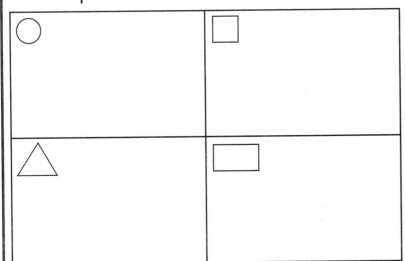

Show 17 both ways.

tally marks

draw objects

Count on. Write the missing numbers.

15, _____ , _____ ,

_____ , 19, _____ ,

_____ , 22, _____

Complete the sentence.

[ ]

A _____ has _____ sides.

Trace the number. Count the objects.

Draw the missing part.

4 = [   ] + [• •]

Count and color to 25.

1	2	3	4	5	6	7	8	9	10
11	12	13	14	15	16	17	18	19	20
21	22	23	24	25	26	27	28	29	30
31	32	33	34	35	36	37	38	39	40
41	42	43	44	45	46	47	48	49	50
51	52	53	54	55	56	57	58	59	60
61	62	63	64	65	66	67	68	69	70
71	72	73	74	75	76	77	78	79	80
81	82	83	84	85	86	87	88	89	90
91	92	93	94	95	96	97	98	99	100

Color the two bubbles that make 4.

2   3   1

Color the box that has more.

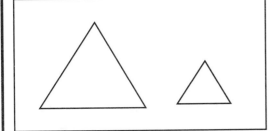   

Draw two lines to connect opposite corners. How many triangles do you see?

_____

Circle the shape that is different.

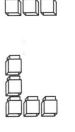

Draw two rectangles.

Color the two dominoes that make 14.

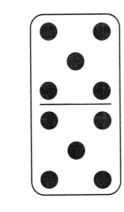   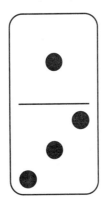   

How many paperclips long is the screwdriver?

_____

Draw a shape that can be made with the smaller shapes.

Match each shape to a real-world object.

Color 2 stars green and 2 stars blue. Write how many stars there are altogether.

_____

Circle a group of 10.

Complete the number sentences.

14 = 10 + _____

_____ + 10 = 14

Color the shapes with no sides.

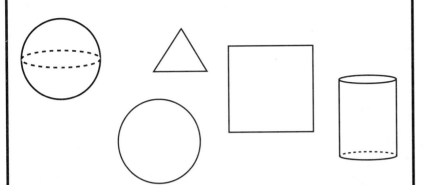

Draw things that are squares. Draw things that are not squares.

Squares	Not Squares

Color the small shapes. Underline the big shapes.

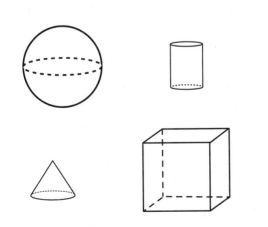

Color the one that can hold more.

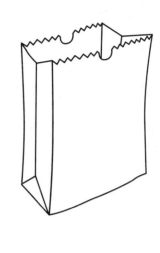

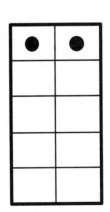

Draw dots to make 10.

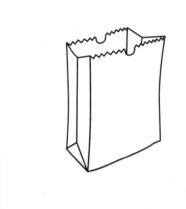

Write a number sentence.

_____ + _____ = _____

---

hexagon

rectangle

A _____

has more sides than a

_____.

Count on. Write the numbers.

16, _____ , _____

How many beetles? _____

How many flies? _____

Circle the set that has more.

Count and color to 26.

1	2	3	4	5	6	7	8	9	10
11	12	13	14	15	16	17	18	19	20
21	22	23	24	25	26	27	28	29	30
31	32	33	34	35	36	37	38	39	40
41	42	43	44	45	46	47	48	49	50
51	52	53	54	55	56	57	58	59	60
61	62	63	64	65	66	67	68	69	70
71	72	73	74	75	76	77	78	79	80
81	82	83	84	85	86	87	88	89	90
91	92	93	94	95	96	97	98	99	100

Draw dots to make ten.

8 + _____ = 10

Color the set that has the least.

Draw a picture to solve the problem.

2 + 3 = _____

Color the correct number of objects.

10

Write the missing 10s.

1	2	3	4	5	6	7	8	9	
11	12	13	14	15	16	17	18	19	
21	22	23	24	25	26	27	28	29	
31	32	33	34	35	36	37	38	39	
41	42	43	44	45	46	47	48	49	

Use **<**, **>**, or **=** to compare.

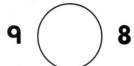

Finish the calendar.

S	M	Tu	W	Th	F	Sa
					20	21
22	23	24	25	26	27	28
29	30	31				

Write the missing part.

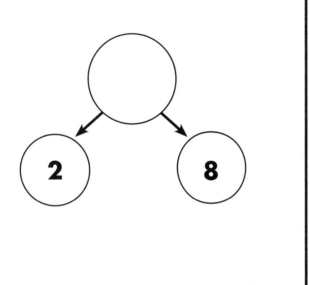

Draw a picture to solve the problem.

Draw a circle. Complete the sentence.

A _____ has _____ sides.

3 + 7 = _____

Draw some blue circles and some yellow circles. How many circles in all?

_____ **+** _____ **=** _____

Draw a set that is equal.

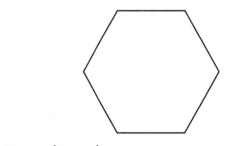

Count by 10s. Color the numbers you say yellow.

1	2	3	4	5	6	7	8	9	10
11	12	13	14	15	16	17	18	19	20
21	22	23	24	25	26	27	28	29	30
31	32	33	34	35	36	37	38	39	40
41	42	43	44	45	46	47	48	49	50
51	52	53	54	55	56	57	58	59	60
61	62	63	64	65	66	67	68	69	70
71	72	73	74	75	76	77	78	79	80
81	82	83	84	85	86	87	88	89	90
91	92	93	94	95	96	97	98	99	100

Use the domino to show 10.

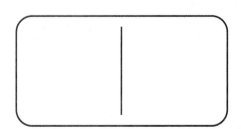

Complete the sentence.

A _____ has

_____ sides.

Draw a picture to solve the problem.

5 + 0 = _____

Draw lines to match each cloud with a rainbow.

Is there an equal number of clouds and rainbows?

yes   **no**

Add 3 triangles to make a rectangle.

Count. Write the numbers

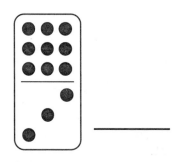 _____ 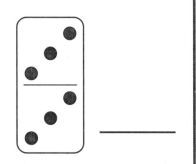 _____

Count and color to 27.

1	2	3	4	5	6	7	8	9	10
11	12	13	14	15	16	17	18	19	20
21	22	23	24	25	26	27	28	29	30
31	32	33	34	35	36	37	38	39	40
41	42	43	44	45	46	47	48	49	50
51	52	53	54	55	56	57	58	59	60
61	62	63	64	65	66	67	68	69	70
71	72	73	74	75	76	77	78	79	80
81	82	83	84	85	86	87	88	89	90
91	92	93	94	95	96	97	98	99	100

Write two numbers to make the statement true.

_____ **is greater than** _____ .

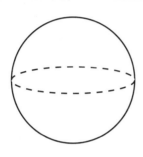

Complete the sentence.

A _____ has _____ sides

and _____ vertices.

Color each space with a sum of 5 to help the crab find his shell.

4 + 1	2 + 2
2 + 3	5 + 1
5 + 0	0 + 5
4 + 2	1 + 4
3 + 3	3 + 2

Draw more tally marks to show 10.

There are 5 houses on Ben's road. There are 2 houses on Ava's road. How many houses are there altogether?

_____ houses

Circle the glass that is full.

Count. Write each number.

_____   _____   _____   _____

_____   _____   _____   _____

_____   _____   _____   _____

_____   _____   _____   _____

_____   _____   _____   _____

Use the dice to show 10.

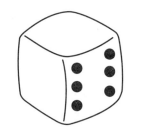 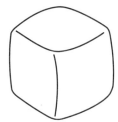

_____ + _____ = 10

Color the bowl with the least number of goldfish.

Color two petals that add to the sum in the center of the flower.

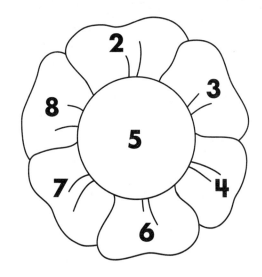

Use the domino to show 5.

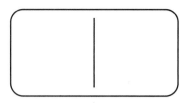

_____ **+** _____ **= 5**

Are the sets equal? If yes, circle the **=**. If no, draw an **X** on the **=**.

Cross out balloons to show the number sentence.

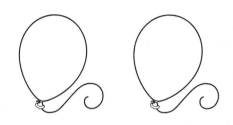

4 – 1 = 3

Show the subtraction problem on the five frame.

5 – 1 = 4

Write the number that is one more.

15, _____

16, _____

Draw a treasure map using any shapes you know.

What shape is it?

circle

square

cone

Color the same amount in each set.

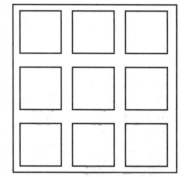

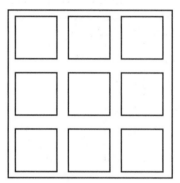

How many legs does one frog have?

_____

Count and color to 28.

1	2	3	4	5	6	7	8	9	10
11	12	13	14	15	16	17	18	19	20
21	22	23	24	25	26	27	28	29	30
31	32	33	34	35	36	37	38	39	40
41	42	43	44	45	46	47	48	49	50
51	52	53	54	55	56	57	58	59	60
61	62	63	64	65	66	67	68	69	70
71	72	73	74	75	76	77	78	79	80
81	82	83	84	85	86	87	88	89	90
91	92	93	94	95	96	97	98	99	100

Four frogs were in the pond. Two frogs jumped out. How many frogs are left?

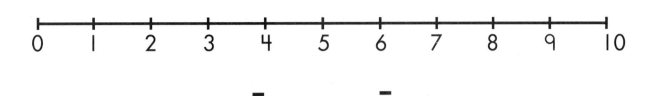

_____ - _____ = _____

There were 3 bluebirds in a tree. Then, 2 more bluebirds flew in. How many birds are in the tree?

_____ + _____ = _____

Write the missing parts.

whole	
5	
part	**part**
4	

whole	
part	**part**
2	2

5 – 0 = _____

Color 4 frogs yellow and 1 frog green.

_____ + _____ = _____

Write numbers to make the number sentence true.

_____ + _____ = 10

The apple tree had 5 apples. A deer ate 2 apples. How many apples are left?

_____ apples

Write a number sentence.

_____ + _____ = _____

Use pattern blocks to draw a caterpillar.

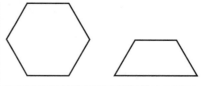

_____

Color 6 bugs yellow and 1 bug green.

_____ + _____ = _____

How many?

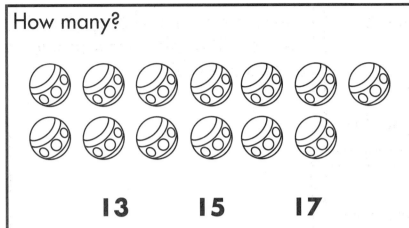

13   15   17

How many bracelets altogether?

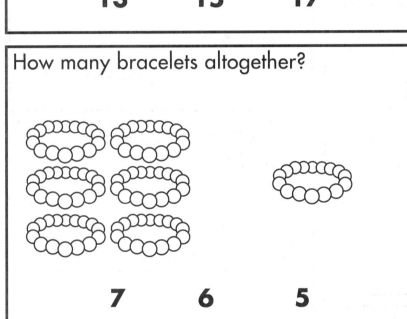

7   6   5

How long?

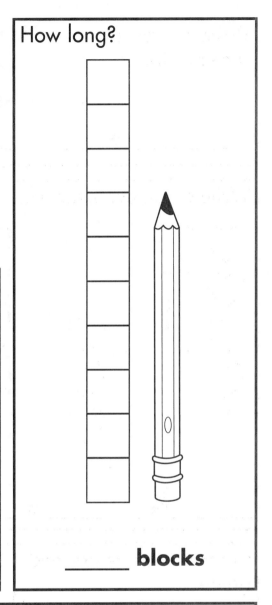

_____ **blocks**

Color the two bubbles that make 6.

Color 5 circles blue and 6 circles yellow.

_____ + _____ = _____

Use two colors to show the number sentence.

2 + 8 = _____

Cross out objects to show the number sentence.

3 − 2 = 1

There are 7 cookies on Lee's plate. There are 3 cookies on Molly's plate. How many cookies altogether?

_____ **cookies**

Count and color to 29.

1	2	3	4	5	6	7	8	9	10
11	12	13	14	15	16	17	18	19	20
21	22	23	24	25	26	27	28	29	30
31	32	33	34	35	36	37	38	39	40
41	42	43	44	45	46	47	48	49	50
51	52	53	54	55	56	57	58	59	60
61	62	63	64	65	66	67	68	69	70
71	72	73	74	75	76	77	78	79	80
81	82	83	84	85	86	87	88	89	90
91	92	93	94	95	96	97	98	99	100

10 and 2 more is _____.

10 and 6 more is _____.

Color the blocks with two colors. Write a number sentence to match.

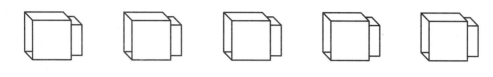

_____ + _____ = _____

Draw lines to make a cube.

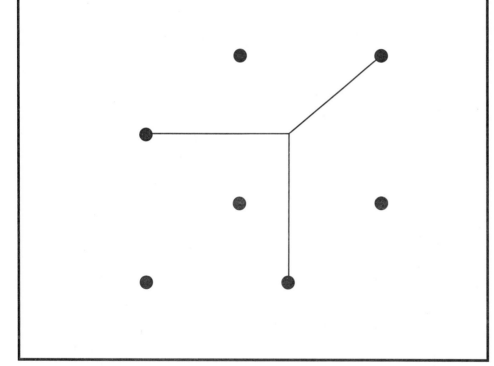

Color the correct number of objects.

12

Circle the one that is the lightest.

$5 +$ $= 8$ $7 +$ $= 9$

What number is ? _____

What number is ? _____

3 + 2 = _____

4 + 1 = _____

How many legs do three chickens have?

_____

Write the missing part.

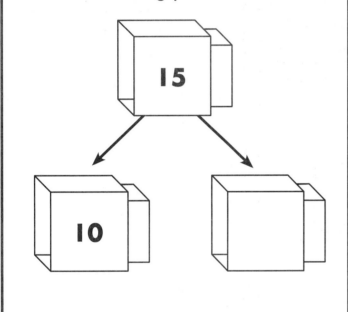

Color the shapes with 4 sides. Draw an **X** on the shapes that do not have 4 sides.

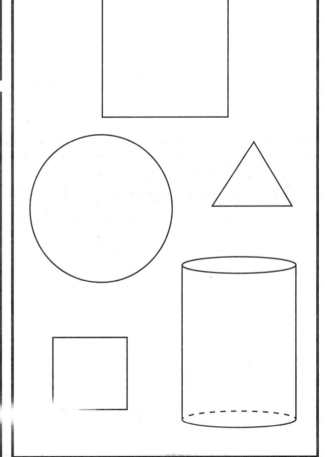

A square has _____ sides and _____ corners.

Write the missing parts.

whole	
10	
part	**part**
6	

whole	
10	
part	**part**
5	

Use rectangles, circles, and squares to draw a person.

Show the subtraction problem on the five frame.

3 – 2 = _____

Kim has 6 candles on her birthday cake. Next year she will add 1 more. How many candles will she have next year?

_____ **candles**

Write a number sentence about the ten frames.

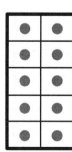 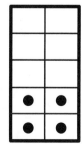

_____ **+** _____ **=** _____

A star has _____ sides

and _____ corners.

How many more to make 10?

There are 8 tomatoes on Chloe's salad.
There are 4 tomatoes on Sally's salad.
How may tomatoes altogether?

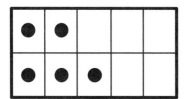

_____

_____

Color the two bubbles that make 7.

Count and color to 30.

1	2	3	4	5	6	7	8	9	10
11	12	13	14	15	16	17	18	19	20
21	22	23	24	25	26	27	28	29	30
31	32	33	34	35	36	37	38	39	40
41	42	43	44	45	46	47	48	49	50
51	52	53	54	55	56	57	58	59	60
61	62	63	64	65	66	67	68	69	70
71	72	73	74	75	76	77	78	79	80
81	82	83	84	85	86	87	88	89	90
91	92	93	94	95	96	97	98	99	100

Cross out bananas to show the number sentence.

5 − 1 = 4

There were 3 shirts in the basket. Sam put 4 more shirts in the basket. How many shirts are in the basket now?

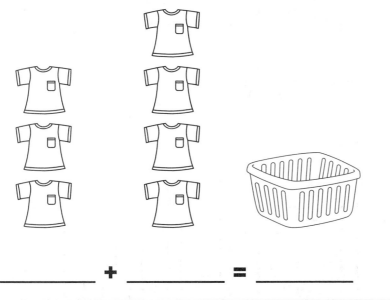

_____ + _____ = _____

How many more to make 10?

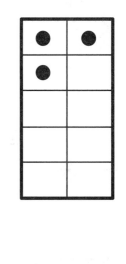

_____

Circle a group of ten.

____ **ten and**

____ **ones =** ____

There were 6 girls playing ball. Then, 3 girls went inside. How many girls were left?

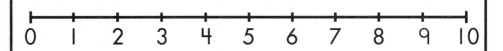

_____ − _____ = _____

Color the two squares that make 4.

| 3 | 3 | 1 |

Use two numbers to make 15.

10   5   7   4

_____ + _____ = 15

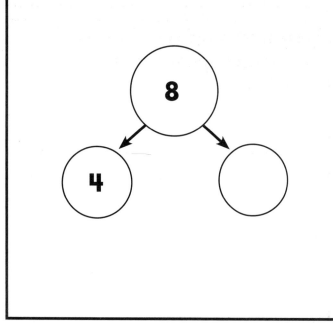

_____ + _____ = _____

How long?

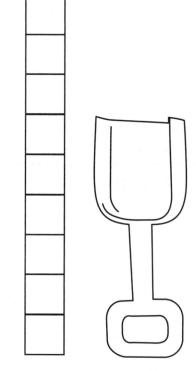

_____ blocks

Write in the missing part.

8

4

How many?

_____

Write the number sentence that tells about the picture.

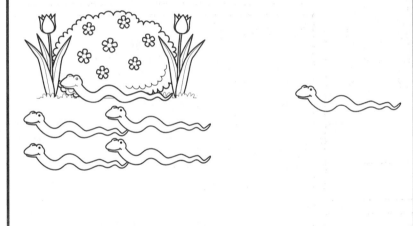

_____

How many children altogether?

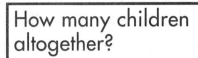

2 + 2 = _____

Circle a group of ten.

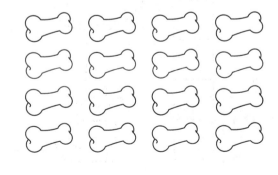

_____ **ten and** _____ **ones**

= _____

Ruby had 6 apples. She ate 2. How many apples does Ruby have left?

Color 10 red and 10 purple. How many did you color?

_____ + _____ = _____

There are 9 horses on Bill's farm. There are 5 horses on Jessica's farm. How many horses are there in all?

Circle a group of 10.

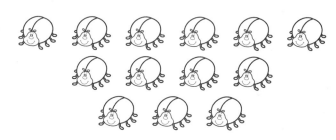

_____ ten and _____ ones = _____

Cross out objects to show the number sentence.

10 − 4 = 6

Count and color to 31.

1	2	3	4	5	6	7	8	9	10
11	12	13	14	15	16	17	18	19	20
21	22	23	24	25	26	27	28	29	30
31	32	33	34	35	36	37	38	39	40
41	42	43	44	45	46	47	48	49	50
51	52	53	54	55	56	57	58	59	60
61	62	63	64	65	66	67	68	69	70
71	72	73	74	75	76	77	78	79	80
81	82	83	84	85	86	87	88	89	90
91	92	93	94	95	96	97	98	99	100

Cross out stars to show the number sentence.

$4 - 1 = 3$

How many tens and ones?

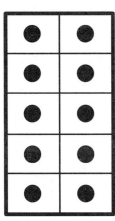 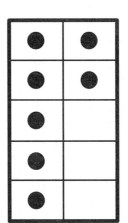

_____ ten and _____ ones = _____

Find the whole.

whole	
part	**part**
3	4

whole	
part	**part**
5	9

Write the missing numbers.

$17 = 10 + \underline{}$

$17 = \underline{} + 7$

$4 + $ $ = 9$ $6 + $ ⭐ $ = 8$

What number is ♥? _____

What number is ⭐? _____

5 – 4 = _____

4 – 2 = _____

Circle the cube that is dark.

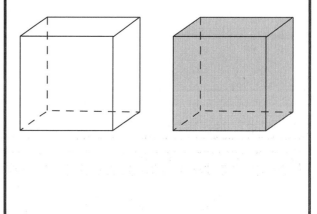

Cross out kites to show the number sentence.

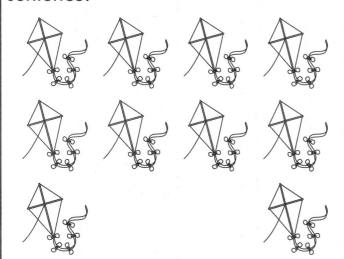

10 – 2 = 8

Draw 20 bubbles.

Add.

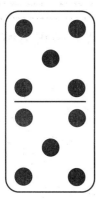 

10 + 3 = _____

Mark has 4 marbles. Jose gives him 3 more. How many marbles does Mark have now?

How long?

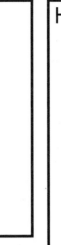

Color the two balloons that make 10.

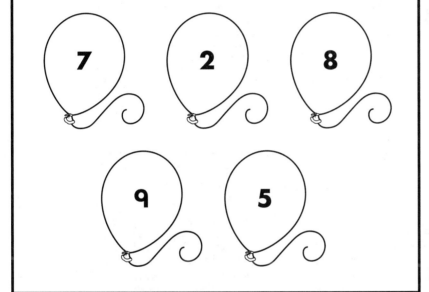

7   2   8

9   5

_____ **blocks**

Write the number sentence that tells about the picture.

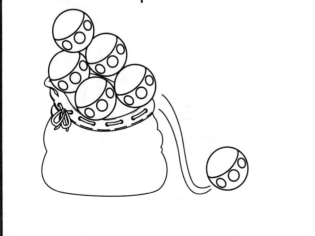

_____

Cross out objects to show the number sentence.

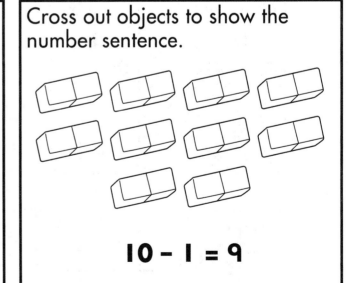

10 – 1 = 9

Draw some purple circles and some green circles. How many circles do you have altogether?

_____ + _____ = _____

How many more to make 10?

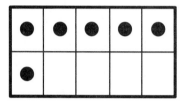

_____

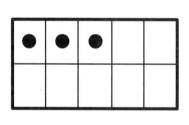

_____

Color the hole that the cone will fit through.

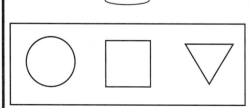

Write the missing part.

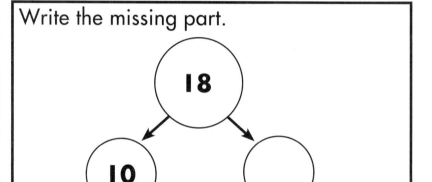

Count and color to 32.

1	2	3	4	5	6	7	8	9	10
11	12	13	14	15	16	17	18	19	20
21	22	23	24	25	26	27	28	29	30
31	32	33	34	35	36	37	38	39	40
41	42	43	44	45	46	47	48	49	50
51	52	53	54	55	56	57	58	59	60
61	62	63	64	65	66	67	68	69	70
71	72	73	74	75	76	77	78	79	80
81	82	83	84	85	86	87	88	89	90
91	92	93	94	95	96	97	98	99	100

How many?

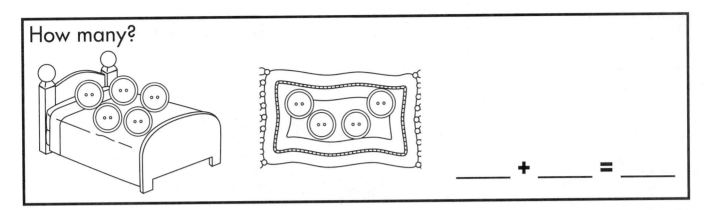

_____ + _____ = _____

There are 5 candles on one cake and 4 candles on the other cake. Draw candles to find how many candles altogether.

_____ **candles**

Count how many.

_____ **ten and**

_____ **one = _____**

Write the missing part.

whole	
8	
part	**part**
7	

Cross out objects to show the number sentence.

4 − 3 = 1

Name _____

Color the two spheres that make 5.

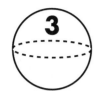 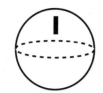 

Show the subtraction problem on the five frame.

$$5 - 3 = 2$$

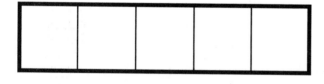

Color the two dice that make 10.

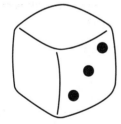 

How many altogether?

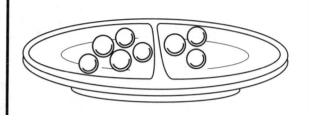

$$5 + 3 = \underline{\hspace{2cm}}$$

How many legs do 5 horses have?

_____

Write the missing parts.

whole	
9	
part	**part**
4	

whole	
part	**part**
1	6

Color the correct number of blocks.

I I

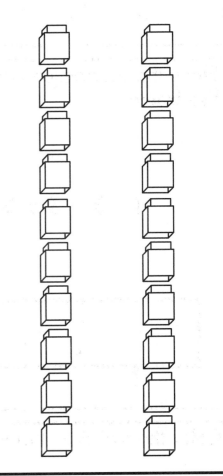

Ben put 10 marbles on the table. Some marbles rolled onto the floor. Draw a picture to tell about the story.

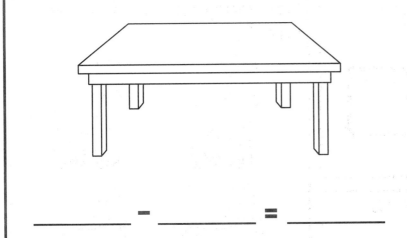

_____ - _____ = _____

Draw dots to make 10.

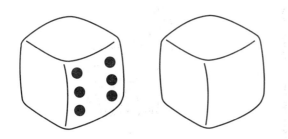

10 = _____ + _____

Color 4 triangles blue.
Color 1 triangle green.

_____ + _____ = _____

Color the correct number of blocks.

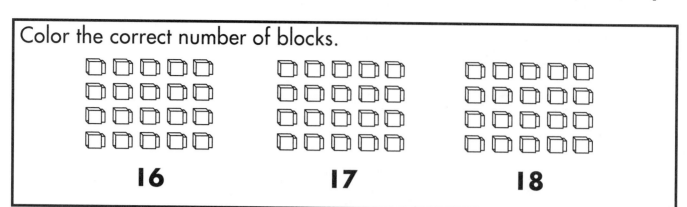

16   **17**   **18**

How long?

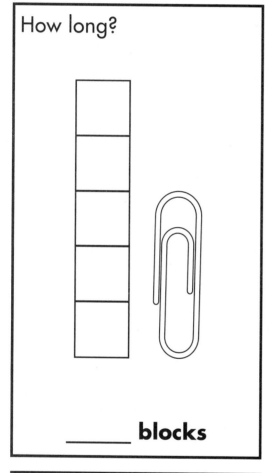

_____ **blocks**

Nina has 5 pieces of gum. She gave 2 to Liv. How many pieces of gum does Nina have left?

_____ **pieces of gum**

Color the two bubbles that make 10.

Count and color to 33.

1	2	3	4	5	6	7	8	9	10
11	12	13	14	15	16	17	18	19	20
21	22	23	24	25	26	27	28	29	30
31	32	33	34	35	36	37	38	39	40
41	42	43	44	45	46	47	48	49	50
51	52	53	54	55	56	57	58	59	60
61	62	63	64	65	66	67	68	69	70
71	72	73	74	75	76	77	78	79	80
81	82	83	84	85	86	87	88	89	90
91	92	93	94	95	96	97	98	99	100

Write the number that comes next in each pair.

 19    10    16

Color 4 balloons red. Color 6 balloons blue.
Write the number sentence.

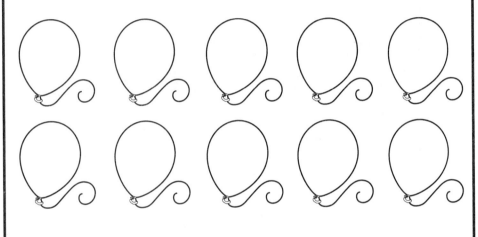

_____ + _____ = 10

I have 3 coins.
How many more
to make 5?

3 + _____ = 5

Cross out objects
to show the
number sentence.

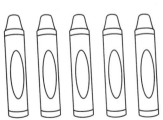

5 − 3 = 2

Add a triangle to form a rectangle.

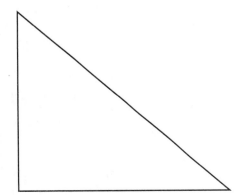

Circle the number sentences that make 10.

5 + 5   2 + 8

4 + 4   3 + 7

Color the 3-D shapes.

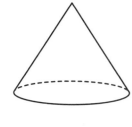
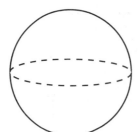

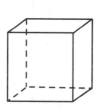

Karla had 2 pencils in her backpack. She gave 1 away. How many pencils does Karla have left?

_____ - _____ = _____

Solve each problem.

2 – 2 = _____

4 – 2 = _____

5 – 5 = _____

2 – 0 = _____

5 – 3 = _____

3 – 1 = _____

Write the missing parts.

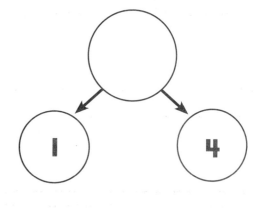

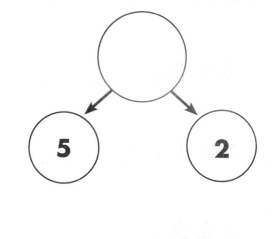

$1 +$  $= 5$ $2 +$ $= 7$

What number is ? _____

What number is ? _____

Draw more circles to make 6 altogether.

_____ + _____ = 6

Write a number sentence to make 10.
Show it on the number line.

_____ + _____ = _____

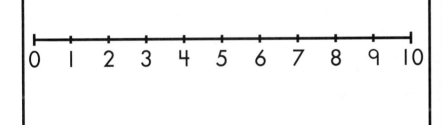

Write the missing numbers.

$4 = 0 +$ _____

$4 = 1 +$ _____

$4 = 2 +$ _____

How many more petals does the flower need to make 10?

_____

Does the number sentence match the ten frame?

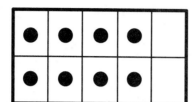

$$6 + 4 = 10$$

yes   **no**

Use rectangles and triangles to draw a rocket ship.

Color the squares that have a sum of 7.

6 + 1	2 + 2	3 + 2
5 + 1	4 + 2	4 + 3

Count and color to 34.

1	2	3	4	5	6	7	8	9	10
11	12	13	14	15	16	17	18	19	20
21	22	23	24	25	26	27	28	29	30
31	32	33	34	35	36	37	38	39	40
41	42	43	44	45	46	47	48	49	50
51	52	53	54	55	56	57	58	59	60
61	62	63	64	65	66	67	68	69	70
71	72	73	74	75	76	77	78	79	80
81	82	83	84	85	86	87	88	89	90
91	92	93	94	95	96	97	98	99	100

Cross out objects to show the number sentence.

$$10 - 6 = 4$$

Color the shapes that have a difference of 4.

4 – 0   5 – 1   4 – 1   5 – 4

How many balls are outside of the basket? _____

How many are in the basket? _____

How many balls altogether? _____

_____ + _____ = _____

Cross out dogs to show the number sentence.

4 – 2 = 2

Circle a group of ten.

____ **ten and**

____ **ones =** ____

1 + = 10   9 + 🜄 = 10

What number is ? _____

What number is 🜄 ? _____

Write the number sentence.

_____ + _____ = _____

Show 20 both ways.

tally marks

draw objects

Does the number sentence match the ten frame?

5 + 5 = 10

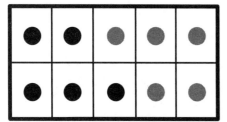

yes   no

Circle the number sentences that have a sum of 9.

5 + 4

2 + 6

3 + 6

3 + 7

8 + 1

Use two colors to show different ways to make ten.

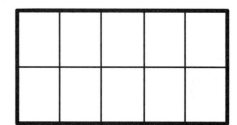

_____ + _____ = 10

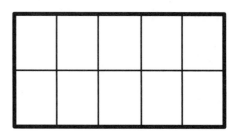

_____ + _____ = 10

Write a number sentence that matches the ten frame.

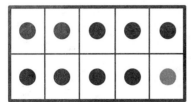

_____ + _____ = _____

How many coins are inside the piggy bank? _____

How many coins are outside of the piggy bank? _____

How many coins altogether? _____

_____ + _____ = _____

How long?

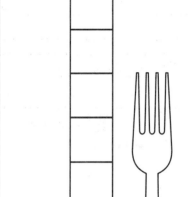

_____ **blocks**

Darius bought 7 cans of soup. He gave 3 cans of soup to his grandmother. How many cans of soup does he have left?

_____ **cans of soup**

Write the missing part.

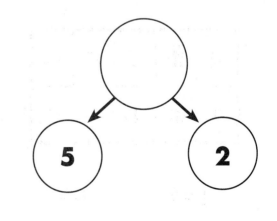

Cross out objects to show the number sentence.

10 − 5 = 5

Color each space with a sum of 6 to help the boy find his puppy.

2 + 1	0 + 6
3 + 3	4 + 2
5 + 1	3 + 2
6 + 0	1 + 4
2 + 4	4 + 3
1 + 5	2 + 5

7 + _____ = 10

9 + _____ = 10

Count and color to 35.

1	2	3	4	5	6	7	8	9	10
11	12	13	14	15	16	17	18	19	20
21	22	23	24	25	26	27	28	29	30
31	32	33	34	35	36	37	38	39	40
41	42	43	44	45	46	47	48	49	50
51	52	53	54	55	56	57	58	59	60
61	62	63	64	65	66	67	68	69	70
71	72	73	74	75	76	77	78	79	80
81	82	83	84	85	86	87	88	89	90
91	92	93	94	95	96	97	98	99	100

Draw more tally marks to make 10.

||||

Solve the problem. Write the sum.

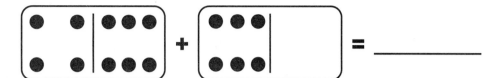 + = _____

Write the missing parts.

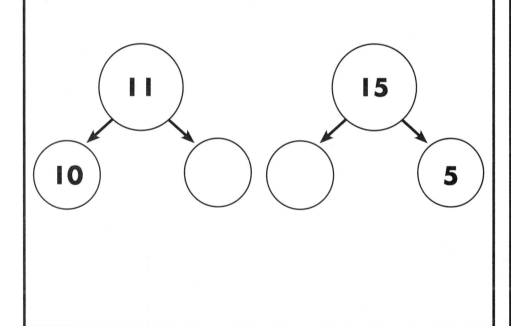

How many legs do 3 cats have altogether?

_____

Cross out moons to show the number sentence.

7 – 2 = 5

Circle the two bees that make 10.

_____ + _____ = _____

10 and 1 more is _____ .

10 and 7 more is _____ .

Draw 2 ways to show this number sentence.

5 + 4 = 9

There were 7 dogs playing. Then, 1 more dog came out to play. How many dogs altogether? Circle the number sentence that matches the word problem.

 **7 + 1 = 8**

5 + 5 = 10

4 + 5 = 9

How many bugs are in the net?

_____

How many bugs are outside of

the net? _____

How many bugs in all?

_____

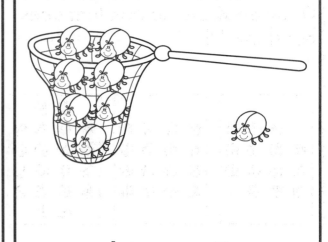

How many crayons altogether?

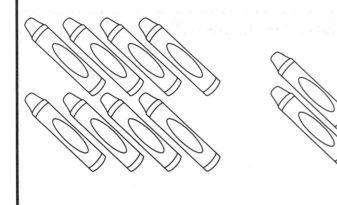

7   8   10

_____ + _____ = _____

Draw dots to make 10.

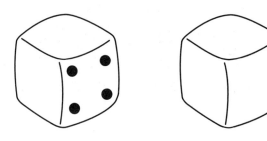

_____ + _____ = **10**

Write a number to make 10 in each set.

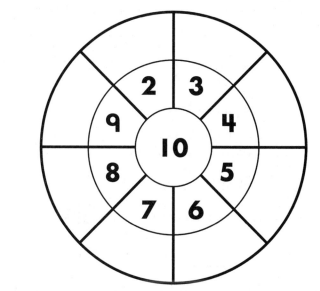

Circle the sets of shapes that can be used to build the hexagon.

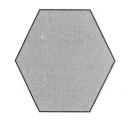

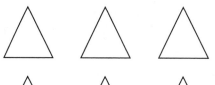

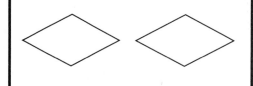

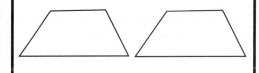

Draw an **X** on the box that does not show 16.

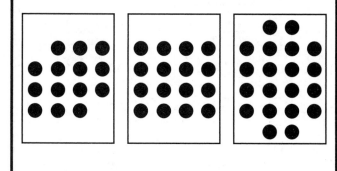

Draw a shape with 3 sides.

Write numbers to make 10. Draw a picture to match the number sentence.

_____ + _____ = **10**

Circle the number sentences that have a sum of 10.

8 + 2

6 + 2

6 + 3

7 + 3

Draw a shape using the two shapes.

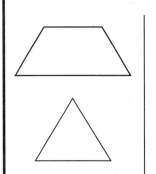

Count and color to 36.

1	2	3	4	5	6	7	8	9	10
11	12	13	14	15	16	17	18	19	20
21	22	23	24	25	26	27	28	29	30
31	32	33	34	35	36	37	38	39	40
41	42	43	44	45	46	47	48	49	50
51	52	53	54	55	56	57	58	59	60
61	62	63	64	65	66	67	68	69	70
71	72	73	74	75	76	77	78	79	80
81	82	83	84	85	86	87	88	89	90
91	92	93	94	95	96	97	98	99	100

Write the missing part.

whole	
part	**part**
5	2

Write the missing numbers.

8 = 0 + _____   8 = 1 + _____   8 = 2 + _____

Show 12 on the ten frames.

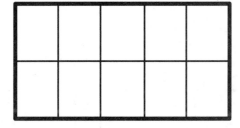

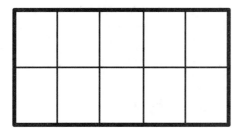

Circle the number sentences that have a difference of 2.

5 – 4

4 – 2

1 – 0

3 – 2

3 – 1

5 – 3

Create your own number sentence.

♡ ♡ ♡ ♡
♡ ♡ ♡ ♡
♡ ♡ ♡ ♡
♡

___ + ___ = ___

Write a number sentence to match the ten frames.

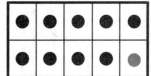

_____ + _____ = _____

Circle the number sentences that have a sum of 9.

$$5 + 5 \qquad 7 + 2$$

$$4 + 5 \qquad 6 + 3$$

Show 11 both ways.

tally marks	draw objects

Draw a picture to find the missing number.

$$11 = 10 + \underline{\qquad}$$

Draw lines to match 2-D shapes with the related 3-D shapes.

Trace the number. Count the objects.

Carlos has 3 eggs. How many more eggs does Carlos need to make 7?

_____ **eggs**

How long?

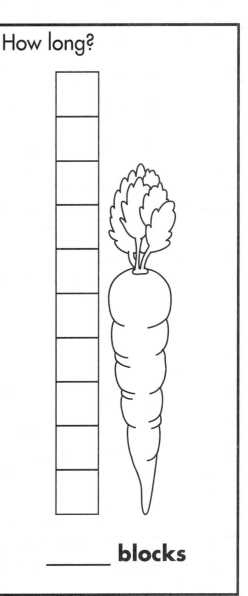

_____ **blocks**

Draw a line to show how many.

10 + 3 = ⬤⬤⬤⬤⬤⬤⬤⬤⬤⬤⬤⬤⬤

10 + 1 = ⬤⬤⬤⬤⬤⬤⬤⬤⬤⬤⬤⬤⬤⬤

10 + 5 = ⬤⬤⬤⬤⬤⬤⬤⬤⬤⬤⬤

Color the two boxes that make 11.

8	5
3	4

How many tens and ones?

_____ **ten and** _____ **ones**

= _____

Show 13 on the ten frames.

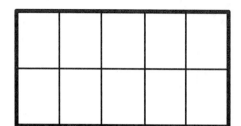

Color each space with a sum of 7 to match the pair of shoes.

6 + 1	3 + 4
0 + 2	5 + 2
2 + 5	0 + 7
4 + 3	1 + 6
4 + 2	7 + 0

Write the missing numbers.

13 = 10 + _____

13 = _____ + 3

Count and color to 37.

1	2	3	4	5	6	7	8	9	10
11	12	13	14	15	16	17	18	19	20
21	22	23	24	25	26	27	28	29	30
31	32	33	34	35	36	37	38	39	40
41	42	43	44	45	46	47	48	49	50
51	52	53	54	55	56	57	58	59	60
61	62	63	64	65	66	67	68	69	70
71	72	73	74	75	76	77	78	79	80
81	82	83	84	85	86	87	88	89	90
91	92	93	94	95	96	97	98	99	100

Solve each problem.

4 – 1 = _____

5 – 2 = _____

Show 12 both ways.

tally marks	draw objects

Trace the number. Count the objects.

18

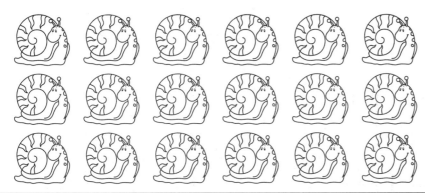

How many?

_____

Count how many.

☺ ☺ ☺ ☺
☺ ☺ ☺ ☺
☺ ☺ ☺

____ **ten and**

____ **one =** ____

Draw things that are rectangles. Draw things that are not a rectangles.

Rectangles	Not Rectangles

Color the correct number of blocks.
13

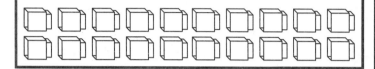

Kit had 9 rings. She gave 3 rings away. How many rings does Kit have left?

_____ **rings**

Complete the sentences with a word or picture.

A _____ is a flat shape.

A _____ is a solid shape.

Color the two boxes that make 12.

7	5

| 3 | 4 |

Show 14 on the ten frames.

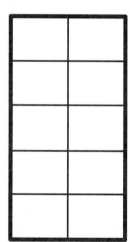

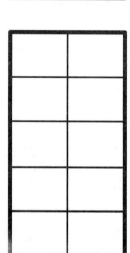

Draw a picture to find the missing number.

15 = 10 + _____

How many?

_____ **birds**

Color the two dominoes that make 16.

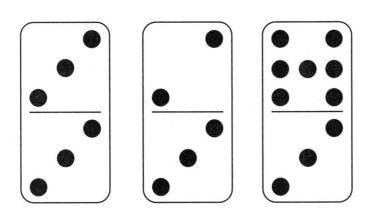

How many tens and ones?

_____ **ten**   _____ **ones**

2 + = 4   3 + = 7

What number is ? _____

What number is ? _____

Circle a group of 10. Complete the number sentences.

15 = 10 + _____   _____ + 10 = 15

Show 14 both ways.

tally marks

draw objects

Complete the shape.

How many sides does it have? _____

Circle the two numbers that make 13.

9   5   3   4

Count and color to 38.

1	2	3	4	5	6	7	8	9	10
11	12	13	14	15	16	17	18	19	20
21	22	23	24	25	26	27	28	29	30
31	32	33	34	35	36	37	38	39	40
41	42	43	44	45	46	47	48	49	50
51	52	53	54	55	56	57	58	59	60
61	62	63	64	65	66	67	68	69	70
71	72	73	74	75	76	77	78	79	80
81	82	83	84	85	86	87	88	89	90
91	92	93	94	95	96	97	98	99	100

How many carrots?

_____

Write the missing parts.

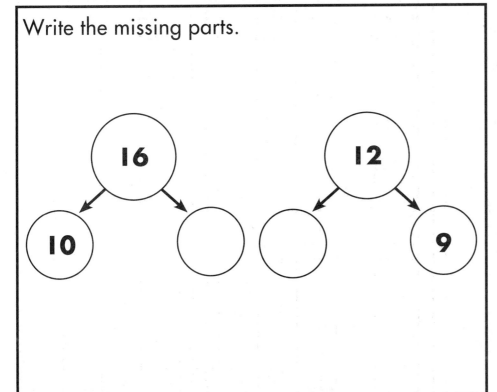

How many legs do 1 dog and 3 geese have altogether?

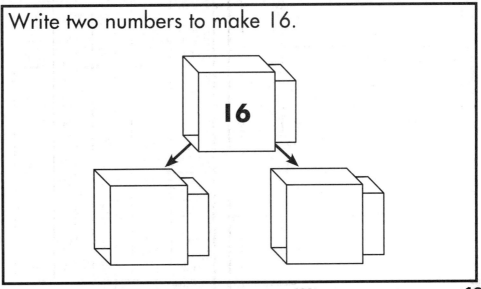

_____

Circle a group of ten.

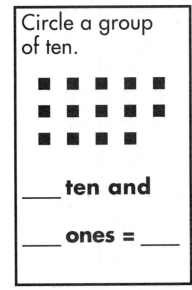

___ ten and

___ ones = ___

Write two numbers to make 16.

16

Circle the number sentences that have a difference of 2.

4 – 3   5 – 3

6 – 4   3 – 2

Color the correct number of blocks.

17

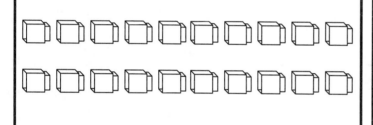

Show 15 on the ten frames.

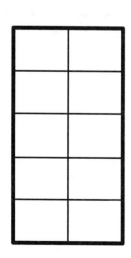

Jose is holding up 5 fingers on one hand and 4 fingers on the other. How many fingers is Jose holding up altogether?

_____ **fingers**

Draw a line to show how many.

10 + 8 =

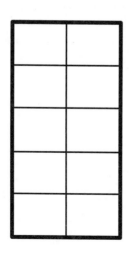

10 + 9 =

10 + 7 =

How many tens and ones in the number 13?

Tens	Ones

Draw a picture to find the missing number.

17 = 10 + _____

Trace the number. Count the objects.

Write the missing numbers.

5 = 0 + _____

5 = 1 + _____

5 = 2 + _____

Show 15 both ways.

tally marks

draw objects

Name _____

Color two dominoes to make 18.

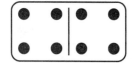 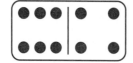 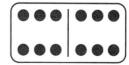

How tall?

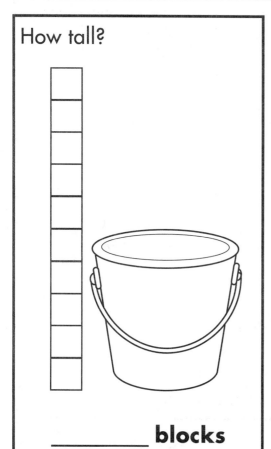

_____ blocks

How many tens and ones in the number 17?

Tens	Ones

Write two different ways to make 10.

_____ + _____ = 10

_____ + _____ = 10

Count and color to 39.

1	2	3	4	5	6	7	8	9	10
11	12	13	14	15	16	17	18	19	20
21	22	23	24	25	26	27	28	29	30
31	32	33	34	35	36	37	38	39	40
41	42	43	44	45	46	47	48	49	50
51	52	53	54	55	56	57	58	59	60
61	62	63	64	65	66	67	68	69	70
71	72	73	74	75	76	77	78	79	80
81	82	83	84	85	86	87	88	89	90
91	92	93	94	95	96	97	98	99	100

Write a number sentence to match the ten frames.

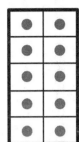 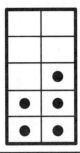

_____ + _____ = _____

Color the hole that the cylinder will fit through.

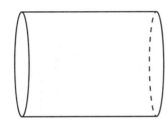

Color the two boxes that make 17.

10	8
5	7

Cross out bugs to show the number sentence.

6 – 2 = 4

3 + = 6   4 + = 8

What number is ? _____

What number is ? _____

How many tens and ones in the number 19?

Tens	Ones

Show 18 on the ten frames.

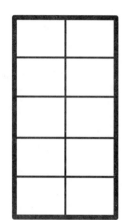

Circle a group of ten. Write the missing numbers.

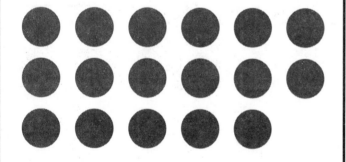

17 = 10 + _____

_____ +7 = 17

Write the missing part.

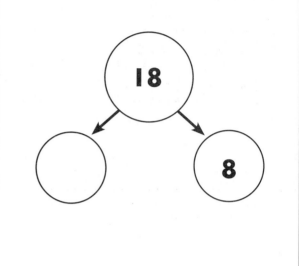

Circle the set of shapes that can be used to build the hexagon.

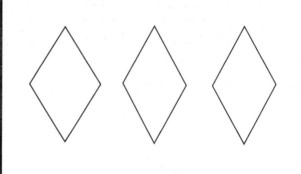

Write a number sentence to match the ten frames.

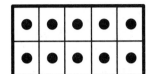

_____ **+** _____ **=** _____

Color the two boxes that make 20.

10		2
	4	
10		9

Color the correct number of circles.

20

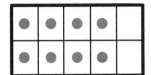

Write the name of the shape.

circle   cube   triangle

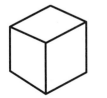

_____

How many tens and ones?

____ ten and ____ ones = ____

Circle a group of 10. Complete the number sentences.

19 = 10 + _____   _____ + 10 = 19

Trace the number. Count the objects.

20

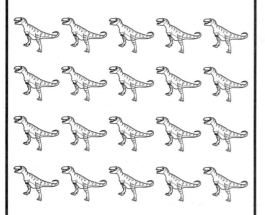

Julia had 8 strawberries. She ate 3. How many strawberries does Julia have left?

_____ **strawberries**

Write the missing numbers.

19 = 10 + _____

19 = 9 + _____

Count and color to 40.

1	2	3	4	5	6	7	8	9	10
11	12	13	14	15	16	17	18	19	20
21	22	23	24	25	26	27	28	29	30
31	32	33	34	35	36	37	38	39	40
41	42	43	44	45	46	47	48	49	50
51	52	53	54	55	56	57	58	59	60
61	62	63	64	65	66	67	68	69	70
71	72	73	74	75	76	77	78	79	80
81	82	83	84	85	86	87	88	89	90
91	92	93	94	95	96	97	98	99	100

0 + 0	0 + 1	0 + 2	0 + 3
0 + 4	0 + 5	1 + 1	1 + 2
1 + 3	1 + 4	2 + 1	2 + 2
2 + 3	3 + 1	3 + 2	4 + 1

3 2 1 0

3 2 5 4

4 3 5 4

5 5 4 5

5 − 0	5 − 1	5 − 2	5 − 3
5 − 4	5 − 5	4 − 0	4 − 1
4 − 2	4 − 3	4 − 4	3 − 1
3 − 2	2 − 2	2 − 0	1 − 1

2 3 4 5

3 4 0 1

2 0 1 2

0 2 0 1